THE STORY

OF THE HEBREWS

THE STORY
OF THE HEBREWS

by Harold A Guy

J M Dent & Sons Limited
Bedford Street London

Made in Great Britain
at the
Aldine Press Letchworth Herts
for
J M Dent & Sons Limited
Aldine House Bedford Street London

ISBN 0 460 09544 7

Contents

Preface

This book tells the story of a remarkable race of people who started as a group of wandering desert tribes and in the course of centuries became a nation in the Middle East. They were never a numerous people but their importance is out of all proportion to their size. Their ideas have powerfully influenced the minds of men in all ages. Many of the world's greatest thinkers and leading men in the realms of science and literature have been Jews. And we cannot fully understand what is happening today in the Middle East unless we know something of the history of the people who are now citizens of the land of Israel.

For Christians there is another important point. Jesus of Nazareth was a Jew and his first disciples belonged to the same race. The Christian world thus owes a great debt to the Jews. Whether we realise it or not, the lives of all of us are influenced by the two great religions of Judaism and Christianity which came from Palestine.

One of the outstanding things about the Jews is their literature—the Hebrew scriptures which form part of our Bible, in the Old Testament. The narrative told here is based on that record. It may be read through as a story on its own. For those who want to see for themselves what the old writers actually said, there are lists of passages from the Old Testament at the end of each chapter. Many people find the usual version of the Bible, written in old English, difficult to understand. The meaning often becomes much clearer in a more modern translation such as the *New English Bible*, published in 1970.

1

The Old Testament

Most of the story of the Hebrew people is to be found in the Old Testament—the first and much larger part of our Bible. This is not a single book in itself but a collection of many books. We cannot say exactly how many people have contributed to the Old Testament as a whole, for many of the books contain the writings of two or more men. It is an omnibus volume containing several different types of literature—historical records, legends, folk-lore, laws, teaching, preaching, poetry. We will consider each of these briefly in turn.

The *history* in the Old Testament covers a period of about 1300 years—as long as the time that separates us from the days when the Saxons were coming to this country. The historical books tell the story of some nomadic tribesmen known as the Hebrews, or sons of Israel, who settled in the country which in early days was called Canaan and later Palestine. It is the land which is at present divided between the states of Israel and Jordan. These tribes gradually became one nation. They were often attacked by surrounding peoples and had to submit to foreign rule and even oppression. The people who survived all the disasters which befell the nation were eventually known as the Jews.

In the course of their history, many *legends* arose. These are stories about actual people and so may be said to be founded to some extent on fact, but the details are not necessarily reliable. The deeds of a great man tended to become exaggerated in the telling; sometimes stories about one man came to be attached to the name of somebody else. All nations, including our own, have legends mixed up with historical narrative, and some legends about the national heroes of the Hebrews are included in the historical records in the Old Testament.

Folk-lore is a somewhat similar type of material. This consists of stories told about people who may actually have lived, but their deeds are regarded as those of the family or tribe rather than of particular individuals. The heroes of these stories represent different types of people. This applies especially to the early periods of a nation's history. Some of the Old Testament accounts of the earliest Hebrews are often regarded today as folk-lore rather than strict history.

There are also books which deal with *laws*. The distinctive thing about the laws of the Hebrews is that they are set down as the commands of God, not like our laws or Acts of Parliament, which are the result of deliberation by men. For the Hebrews, as for most ancient peoples, their religion ruled their life and God was thought to be concerned with every part of it. There are hundreds of rules and regulations in the Old Testament which the Jews were expected to observe. Some books are given over almost entirely to these, but there are also laws of various kinds scattered among other books which deal with history or teaching.

Much of the *teaching* in the Old Testament is contained in the books of the prophets. These were not, as some people imagine, men who tried to foretell the future. Most of what they had to say was directly related to the people of their own time. They spoke or wrote about God and his relations with men and the sort of conduct which people ought to practise. Their words were written down either by the prophets themselves or by their followers. There are three large books of the prophets in the Old Testament and a dozen smaller ones. Some of these books include the teaching of more than one prophet. The prophets were a great influence among the Hebrews over a period of about 400 years.

There is also *poetry* in the Old Testament. One book (Psalms) is a collection of poems and hymns, written by various people at different periods. Eastern poetry does not depend on rhyme and rhythm, as much of our poetry does. Its main feature is repetition. The poet expresses a thought and then repeats it in a different way. This is called parallelism and it occurs in other places besides the Psalms. Some of the teaching of the prophets is in poetic form and the book of Proverbs, a collection of wise sayings, has many examples of parallelism. There is also a long epic poem, with an introduction and an epilogue in prose—the book of Job.

All these books, containing these varying types of literature, were put together and edited over the course of hundreds of years and were finally settled by the Jews of Palestine in the first century A.D. as constituting their sacred literature. They were written in Hebrew, except for a few portions in a dialect called Aramaic. (There were also other books, written in Greek, which the Jews of Palestine did not accept as being on the same level. They are called the Apocrypha.) All this is religious literature. This may tend to put us off, for we think of religious books as a special type, different from those which deal with history or political questions or social affairs. There is plenty about these matters in the Old Testament, but to the Hebrews religion was not a separate aspect of life and thought, but at the centre—something which affected every activity and influenced their whole outlook. This was the case with most peoples in the ancient world and is still true of many eastern nations. The most important thing for them was the relation between the nation and God. This determined their view of history and the form which their laws and teaching took. All the books of the Old Testament were written from this point of view.

This collection of Hebrew literature should more correctly be referred to as the Old Covenant. Covenant is a word meaning a compact or agreement. It is used of legal documents and treaties between nations and sometimes of arrangements between business companies. The Hebrews described the relation between the nation and God as a covenant, by which the people undertook to keep faithful to him and he promised to look after them. This is the theme of the Old Testament. The New Testament, the second part of our Bible, is based on a new covenant between God and men, which was brought about by Jesus. We use the word 'testament' because the Greek word for covenant was translated into Latin by *testamentum*.

In the course of their long history the ideas of the Hebrews on many subjects naturally changed. If people are to progress their ideas must develop and this applies to religion as well as other matters. In studying each period of the history of the Hebrews and Jews, we must notice the thoughts which they had about God and his nature and about the attitude of men towards God.

The methods of writing books in ancient times were not the same as those we use today. A modern historian has at hand several different types of material about the period he wishes to write about—documents coming from that time, comments on these by scholars, accounts of other historians in books or magazines, newspaper articles and perhaps government reports. He consults all these, arranges the facts and the different opinions, and then writes a book in his own words, giving his own ideas on the subject. He shows how he has used the material available to him, by stating in what ways he is indebted to previous writers on the subject. If he quotes or refers to another writing he acknowledges it. There are laws of copyright which make it an offence to give extracts from somebody else's work without acknowledgment.

A writer in ancient times was in quite a different situation. He often had little else to go on other than a number of stories and legends, some of which had been told by word of mouth for a very long time and had never been written down. If he had access to written narratives, he sometimes copied these out almost word for word. There was no law of copyright and he probably did not know who had drawn up the account he was using. He might put alongside this some oral traditions which he had heard. He sometimes added his own comments here and there, but gave no indication where the matter in his sources stopped and his own words began. Scholars today try to find this out by examining the style and vocabulary and the different ideas expressed. The ancient historian should thus be regarded as an editor or compiler rather than an author. Sometimes he had two accounts of the same historical period or two versions of a particular event. He could adopt one of two courses. He might put down both accounts, one after the other. This is why in some places in the Old Testament a story seems to be told twice over. We shall see that in the book called Judges there are two accounts of the invasion of Palestine by the Hebrew tribes and that there are two stories of the way in which David was introduced to the court of king Saul. The other method was to use the two accounts, running them together to make one narrative. Thus the story of the bad feeling between Joseph and his brothers was told in two versions, which differed in several respects, and the editor of the book of Genesis ran the two together to

5

make one connected narrative. In these instances it is possible for us to disentangle the two sources and see that each, taken by itself, makes a quite intelligible story.

The first book of the Old Testament is called Genesis— a Greek word which means birth or beginning. Before the actual narratives about the Hebrews begin (in chapter 12), there are a number of stories which we call myths. 'Myth' is a word which is often misunderstood; it is not, as some people imagine, a kind of fairy story told simply to entertain. Myths are stories which attempted to explain the beliefs and customs of a nation or race. They tried to show how these arose in early ages and in most myths God (or the gods) played an important part. Today we regard them as poetic narratives, not as statements of historical facts. Many ancient peoples had creation-myths, which gave their ideas of how the world came into being. These were necessarily mostly speculation, for they had not our scientific knowledge about the nature and size of the universe. The ancient Chinese thought that every-thing came originally from a great egg, out of which a god emerged who used the shell of the egg to make the world. An Egyptian myth told of a god who was a potter, who shaped the earth on his wheel. In ancient Babylon there was a story that the world had been created when the gods cut up the body of a monster and from this they formed the earth, sun, moon and stars. Jews who were in exile in Babylon in the sixth century B.C. knew of this story and later they used it as the basis of an account of the creation which is found now in the first chapter of Genesis. But they were offended at some elements in the Babylonian myth, for this related that the gods had been quarrelling and the body of the monster was a goddess who had been killed. So the Jews cut out these unworthy parts and rewrote the story, commencing with the words: 'In the beginning *God* created the heaven and the earth' (*Gen.* 1.1). We can trace the connection with the Babylonian story in some of the words which are used, which are the Hebrew form of Babylonian words. This is not a scientific statement of how the world began and it does not fit in with our idea of the origin of the earth. It is not really an account of the universe as we know it, for it assumes that the earth is flat and over it is a dome from which the stars hang, that there is water above this and underneath the earth and that our world is at the centre, with the sun and moon revolving round it. It is a good example of an early creation-myth, for it explains the world in religious terms, showing it as the result of the activity of God. In that sense it has been said that the early chapters of Genesis 'are not true but are full of truth'. That is why the Jews placed this story at the beginning of their collection of literature, although it was not by any means the first part of the Bible to be written.

The Hebrews had another ancient account of the beginning of the earth and the first animals and men. It was an earlier story than the one they borrowed from the Babylonians, but it comes after the Babylonian one in *Genesis* 2.4. The two creation stories disagree in a number of ways. In one of them fishes and birds and animals are said to have been made first and then man, as the climax of creation (1.20, 1.25, 1.26). In the other story man was the first creature to be made (2.7), before anything else on earth; then trees were made to grow (verse 9) and finally animals, to be companions for man (verse 19). The Hebrew word for man is *adam*, so the first man in this story was called that. The editor of the book of Genesis put the two stories down without attempting to combine them.

These myths were attempts to explain the origin of the world and the human race. Others told of the way in which the social habits and institutions of men came into being. Genesis goes on to narrate the first offence against God (the man and the woman took fruit from a forbidden

7

tree), the first murder (Cain killed his brother Abel), the first musician (Jubal—'the ancestor of those who play the lyre and pipe'—*Gen*. 4.21), the first metal-worker (Tubal-cain—*Gen*. 4.22) and the origin of the different races of the Middle East, said to be descended from the three sons of Noah (*Gen*. 10.32). This man is the hero of a long story about a flood which drowned all creatures and men except those of his own family. Noah made a great boat or ark and in it he put a pair of various species and so preserved the human race and animals. Other peoples beside the Hebrews had a similar story and we can read the Babylonian one from the clay tablets on which it was inscribed. This relates how a man named Ut-napishtim collected men and animals as directed by the gods and set out in a boat when everything else was destroyed by a flood. The river valleys in Babylon were often inundated when the rivers rose, so this myth has some historical basis. In the Babylonian story, after the flood had subsided the necklace of a goddess was hung in the sky as a remembrance of the deliverance of Ut-napishtim. In the Genesis account this is portrayed as a rainbow which appeared as a sign that God would never again flood the earth. We explain the rainbow as caused by the splitting-up of the light of the sun's rays into the colours of the spectrum. Ancient people knew nothing of this but they attempted to account for the rainbow by adding this part to the myth about the flood.

The last myth in these early chapters of Genesis gives an imaginative explanation of why there are different languages. It assumes that once all men used the same speech. They started to build a city and a great tower which would reach up to heaven, but this displeased God, who thought that men were getting too self-assertive. So he upset their speech, so that they could not understand one another. This confusion made them give up their design and they got scattered about in different places.

The teller of the story probably considered it wrong for men to leave their nomadic life and take to living in cities and he thought that their language difficulties were a punishment for this. This myth also has Babylonian connections, for there were great towers built in their cities, which were probably places of sacrifice to the gods and they may have had these in mind when they told the story of this tower of Babel.

In these early stories in Genesis God is often pictured in a very simple and primitive way. Like a man he takes a walk in a garden in the cool of the evening and men can hide themselves from his sight (*Gen.* 3.8). He is jealous because men might become like him (3.22); he thinks that he has made a mistake in creating man and petulantly decides to destroy them. He descends from heaven to see what men are up to and is afraid that they might achieve too much, so that nothing will be impossible for them (11.5, 11.6). As we shall see, the Hebrews eventually came to have an idea of God far superior to the one in these simple stories.

The value of these myths is not in the events which they relate but in the emphasis which they place on the activity of God—although this may be expressed in a rather crude way—and the insistence that men are responsible to God for their actions. This was always one of the keynotes of Hebrew religion and is probably the reason why these stories were preserved and included in their sacred literature.

PASSAGES REFERRED TO IN THIS CHAPTER:

The Hebrew story of the first men: *Genesis* 2.4 to 4.26.
The (later) Babylonian account of the creation: *Genesis* 1 and 2.1 to 2.3.
Noah and the flood: *Genesis* 6.5 to 9.17.
The city and tower of Babel: *Genesis* 11.1 to 11.9.

2

The Early Hebrew Nomads

The Old Testament story opens in the part of the world now known as the Middle East (see map on p. 11). It extends from Egypt in the south west to Iraq and Iran (Persia) in the east. It now includes a number of states which are mostly Arab by race and Muslim by religion. Four thousand years ago this area was inhabited by wandering tribesmen, who trekked from one place to another with their sheep and goats, living in tents which they carried on mules and camels when they moved. The country was rough, in some places desert where the only hope of survival lay in finding an oasis, in other places wild heath land where there were bushes and trees which afforded some shelter from the sun and storms. Sometimes the nomads settled for a period but never for long, soon travelling on to a further district where they could find some kind of pasture and water for their flocks and herds. Their wandering life was a hard and dangerous one. Sometimes different tribes banded together for mutual support and protection. There would be fights between groups for possession of an oasis or pasturing ground or a large powerful tribe might try to oppress a smaller one. They protected themselves from wild animals and human enemies with their sticks and weapons of stone. They

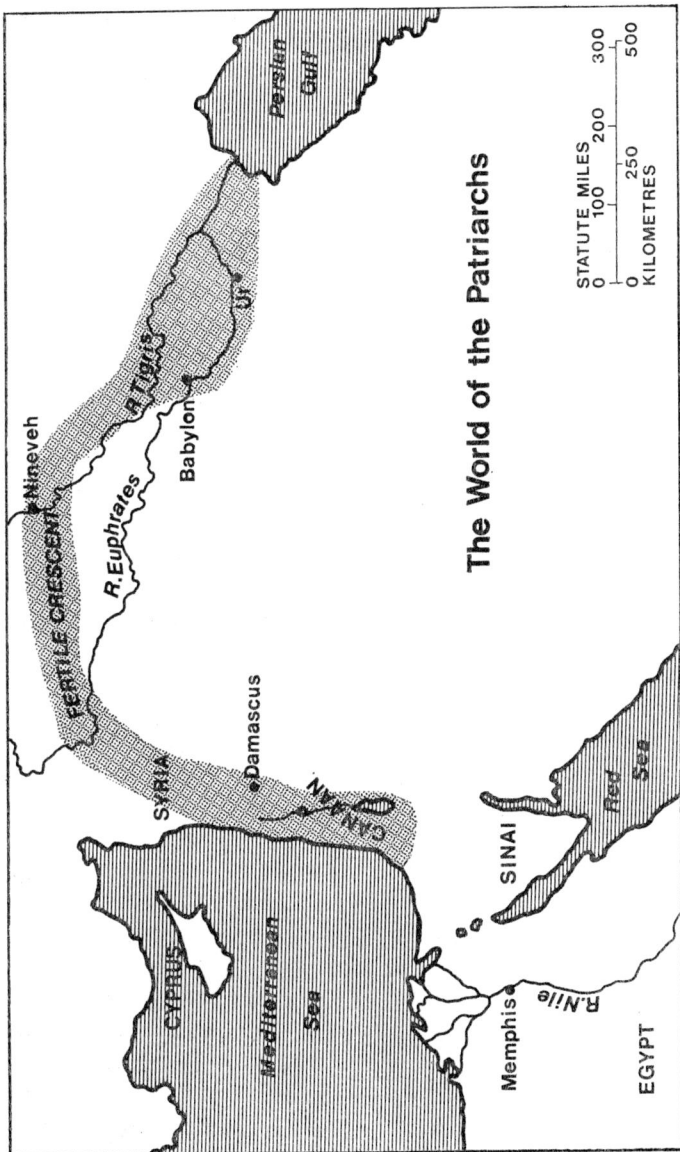

The World of the Patriarchs

STATUTE MILES
0 100 200 300
0 250 500
KILOMETRES

were dark-skinned, short of stature but strong and fierce. They belonged to what is known as the Semitic race.

At both the western and eastern ends of this world of the roving shepherds there were two great centres of civilisation which had been rivals for centuries. Both were situated about great rivers—the Nile in Egypt and the Euphrates and Tigris in Mesopotamia (a name which means 'between the rivers'). The chief cities of Egypt were Memphis (where Cairo now stands) and Thebes further south, up the Nile. The great pyramids which still stand in the desert near Cairo were already hundreds of years old, constructed as tombs for the ancient kings (or Pharaohs, as they were called) of Egypt. The tombs of the kings which have been opened at Luxor, near the former city of Memphis, have revealed something of the splendour and wealth of the ancient Egyptians. In the east the cities of Mesopotamia were Ur on the Euphrates, about 150 miles inland from the Persian Gulf, and Babylon further up that river—not far from the modern city of Baghdad—and Nineveh much further north, on the Tigris. The people who lived in Mesopotamia were Sumerians and their cities, like those of Egypt, were centres of culture and wealth and commerce. Excavations in recent times on the site of Ur have shown that it was a flourishing place with many thousands of people and a high standard of civilisation. We can gain a good picture of the ancient city, with its streets lined with shops and houses, the temples of the gods and the palaces of the rulers.

The district between Mesopotamia and Egypt was traversed by traders as well as the nomadic tribesmen, and travellers generally followed a route which avoided going across the desert. It has been given the name of the Fertile Crescent; it went north-west up the plain between the Euphrates and Tigris, then bore west and south to the district around Damascus—another ancient city, north of

Palestine—then past the lake of Galilee towards the Mediterranean coast and along the coastal plain and the northern edge of the Sinai peninsula into Egypt.

In the desert and around the Fertile Crescent the nomadic shepherds in their wanderings were little concerned with the life in the cities, although some of them did occasionally settle and eventually form villages and towns. A tribe might arrive at a favourable district where the ground was more fertile and they could sow seed. They would have to stay there until the following summer if they wanted to reap a crop and then a further year if they wanted to make use of the ground which they had prepared. Their tents were gradually replaced by more permanent dwellings, huts or houses were built, agriculture was practised and a village or a town grew up. The nomads had become settlers. It was in this way that the cities of Mesopotamia had probably originated, when tribes had come from Asia Minor and Syria into the fertile river valleys and settled down.

There were many differences between the nomads and the people who lived in towns, both in their way of life and in their outlook. The nomads kept their flocks and herds and traded with the wool of their sheep and the hides of their cattle, while the settlers practised agriculture. The nomads lived in tents, while the settlers built houses and shops. The life of the nomads was naturally more rough and dangerous and those who survived were a more hardy and healthy folk than the settlers. Their outlook was more healthy also. They were ruled sternly by the chief of the tribes (or patriarch, a word which means father-and-ruler) and rough justice was administered, but their relations with each other, within the family and the tribe, were fair and their moral life in general was on a higher level than that of the townspeople. In the cities evils developed that often go with a more advanced stage of society—a gulf between the rich and the poor, exploitation of the working people by their employers, unfair practices in trade and commerce, oppression by rulers and kings and slavery.

This difference showed itself also in religion. The nomads kept faithful to their tribal god. Each tribe had its own god, who was thought to travel with them and look after them. They were not monotheists (believers in one God only), for each tribe acknowledged that other tribes had their own gods. Such people who worship one god, while admitting the existence of others, are said to practise not monotheism but monolatry. In addition to believing in the tribal god, the nomads accepted that there were also spirits who had their homes at particular spots such as rivers and streams, rocks, mountains and hills. When they visited such places, they had to be sure that they were on good terms with the god or spirit of the district. But they looked to their own particular tribal god to guide and protect his people.

When nomads became settlers, a number of tribes often joined together to form the new community and their gods became mixed up as well. The inhabitants of the city thus came to acknowledge several gods. They would find no difficulty in this, for they did not think of one God as being all-powerful. The worship of many gods is called polytheism and various practices developed which were unknown in the nomadic state. Temples were built for the gods, where they were thought to dwell and where sacrifices were made in order to gain their favour and ensure the welfare of the people. Priests were appointed for these duties, people who were considered especially qualified to approach the gods on behalf of their worshippers. These men often gained great power over the rulers of the country as well as over the common people. Among the nomads the religious practices were of a more simple kind and the patriarch was generally the priest of the tribal god as well as ruler of the tribe. Polytheism was also generally accompanied by a lower standard of conduct and morality in the cities.

Sometimes groups of people in a city became dissatisfied with the life there and the old urge to wander came upon them again. Then they would pack up their few belongings, load their camels or mules and go into the country or desert and become nomads. One such group left Ur, the chief town of the Chaldean empire, about 1700 B.C., a city which had already been established for over a thousand years. A man named Terah set out with his family and migrated north up the Euphrates to a place called Haran. His son Abraham succeeded to the chieftainship on the death of Terah and he led the tribe westwards until they arrived in the land which was then called Canaan, which we have known as Palestine.

The wandering of Abraham and his people was but one of many movements of tribes of Semites about this time. His tribe came to be known as the Hebrews. The word means 'the other side' and it was probably given to them by the inhabitants of the country to which they came from across a river—either the Euphrates, when they arrived at Haran, or the Jordan, when they got into Canaan. Several stories are told in the book of Genesis about the wanderings of Abraham. He stopped at various places and once went into Egypt for a while, but returned to Canaan. He travelled as far north as Damascus, where the Hebrews fought with another tribe who were trying to establish their rule over the land. Later he is said to have been on the south-west coast, at Gaza. He died and was buried in the south of Canaan.

In telling the stories about Abraham, the Old Testament writers brought out his religious ideas and showed how they influenced his activities. They said that it was at the command of Abraham's God that he left Haran. The account in *Genesis* 12 begins: 'The Lord said to Abraham, "Leave your country and go to a land that I will show you".' The story emphasises that at each place where he stopped Abraham built an altar. This would be a large block of stone on which sacrifices of animals were made. These places became sacred spots to the Hebrews. The relationship between the people and the Hebrew God, who was thought of as being the real unseen head of the tribe, was called a covenant. There is a graphic description in Genesis of a mysterious ceremony in which God is said to have made a covenant with Abraham, promising him that his descendants would live in the land he was then occupying.

Two stories illustrate the character of Abraham. With him was his nephew Lot, who had his section of the tribe to look after. The herdsmen of Lot's cattle used to quarrel with those of Abraham over the rights at an oasis and fights used to break out. There was a danger of a serious split in the community, so Abraham suggested that they should separate and, although he was the senior, he told Lot to choose which part of the land he would take. Lot preferred the fertile Jordan valley, while Abraham had to be content with the more arid district of the south and the mountainous country in the centre of Canaan. The story had an important sequel. Lot and his clansmen eventually moved to the region around the Dead Sea, where two cities, Sodom and Gomorrah, were noted for the evil lives of their inhabitants. The district was devastated not long afterwards by some terrible disaster, probably from a volcanic eruption. The Old Testament writer says that fire rained down from heaven and destroyed the cities. Lot and his family escaped just in time, although his wife was overtaken by the sandstorm in the desert. The writer thought this was a just punishment for the wickedness of the people of these cities. Lot passes out of the story. It was Abraham who remained a nomad and became the ancestor of the Hebrew nation.

The other story about Abraham illustrates the religious

practices of the period. Human sacrifice was carried out in the cities of Mesopotamia and by the people of Canaan among whom Abraham was living. This custom seems to us a cruel and barbarous one, but the thought behind it was that a man wished to give to his god the most precious thing he possessed. So a king or a chief used to kill his first son as an offering. The story in Genesis says that the God of the Hebrews told Abraham to take his son Isaac and offer him as a sacrifice. Animals were sacrificed in this way; after they had been killed, the carcase was burnt on an altar, to show that the offering was completely given up to God, who would be pleased with the gift. This was known as a 'whole burnt offering'. Isaac accompanied his father up a mountain side, carrying the wood for the fire. On arriving at the spot Abraham prepared the altar, bound up Isaac and laid him on it. He had raised his knife to kill his son, when a 'voice' told him to stop, for he had proved his faithfulness to God. He then saw a ram which had been caught in a bush near by and he sacrificed that instead. The story was told probably to illustrate Abraham's loyalty and obedience to the commands of his God. It was also intended as an explanation of how it came about that a ram was used later by the Hebrews in their sacrifices. We can also see in it a dramatic way of telling how Abraham rejected the practice of human sacrifice, although this was the accepted thing in the cities and probably among nomads as well.

After the death of Abraham Isaac became the patriarch of the Hebrew tribes. The main stories about him are concerned with his last years and his sons, Esau and Jacob. Although they were twins, they were very different in temperament and character. Esau is described as 'skilful in hunting, a man of the plains'—a typical open-air nomadic type. Jacob preferred to stay at home—more of the settler type. Esau was his father's favourite, Jacob was his mother's. Two stories illustrate their characters.

Esau once came in from the country, tired and hungry. Jacob was cooking a stew. 'Give me some of that red stuff', demanded Esau. But Jacob refused—'not until you swear that you give me your birthright'. This meant the privileges which he would inherit from his father. Esau agreed. He was rash and impetuous, ready to sacrifice his greatest possession on the impulse of the moment. Jacob appears in this story as a crafty and scheming man, heartless towards his hungry brother.

The other narrative concerns their father Isaac. When he was old and realised that he had not much longer to live, he wished to give his blessing to Esau. He told him to go hunting and kill a deer and cook and bring the meat so that they could eat together. A meal was often held to mark an important event and the giving of the father's blessing was a solemn occasion. Their mother Rebecca overheard what Isaac had said and she determined that Jacob should get the blessing instead. So she told him to take two kids from the flock, which she killed and cooked in preparation for the meal. Then Jacob took the food to his father and pretended to be Esau. Isaac's sight was so bad that he could not tell who it was. When he wondered that the food had been prepared so quickly, Jacob slyly said that God had given him success in his hunting. The old man then bestowed his blessing on Jacob, giving him the rights of the eldest son—lordship over the land and over the family. Soon afterwards Esau returned from his hunting and the father was greatly distressed at the trick that had been played on him. But he could not give Esau any blessing. He could only tell him that he would have a hard life, away from the fertile country. Both these stories illustrate the eastern idea that once a word had been spoken it could not be taken back, whether it was the promise of a birthright or the giving of a blessing. It was as if words were thought of as having a force in themselves, as valid as if they had been put down in a written document.

Esau was so angry that he vowed to kill his brother, so Rebecca sent Jacob away from the estate to stay with his uncle. He went north and after travelling about sixty miles arrived at a district called Luz, in the centre of Palestine. As he slept one night in the open air he dreamed that he saw a staircase or ladder reaching from earth to sky. Everyone at that time thought that the world was flat and that over it was a great dome which was heaven, the place where God (or the gods) lived. If God wanted to communicate with men, he used messengers which are generally called angels. In his dream Jacob saw these moving up and down the stairs and also saw God there, who said: 'I am the God of Abraham and Isaac', and promised to be with Jacob and to give him the land where he was. When Jacob awoke he exclaimed: 'Surely the Lord is in this place and I did not know it! This must be his house'. He was evidently surprised to realise this, for he seems to have thought that in moving from the home of his tribe he had left the God of the Hebrews behind; it was a common idea that the tribal God lived in the territory which his people inhabited. But Jacob was impressed by the fact that his God was still with him, so he set up a stone as a memorial of his experience and called the place Bethel, which means 'House of God'. Long afterwards it became a sacred shrine for the Hebrews. He then made a covenant and promised that he would be faithful if God would protect him and make him prosper.

Jacob was away from his family for a long time, working for his uncle, whose two daughters he married. (Men generally had more than one wife then.) He eventually decided to return home and, afraid of the vengeance of his brother Esau, who was now a powerful chieftain, sent presents to him in advance. Before he met Esau he had another strange experience. He is said to have wrestled all night with a man at a stream at a place called Jabbok and would not let the man go until he had blessed him and told him his name. It was an ancient idea that to know the name of a person or a god was to have some power over him and the man who met Jacob probably represented the god or spirit of the place. Jacob got his blessing and himself received a new name—Israel, which meant 'one who has prevailed with God'. The stories of Jacob at Bethel and at the river are accounts of his experiences and the change in his outlook, described, as was a common practice among eastern story-tellers, in the form of a dramatic narrative.

Next day Jacob met Esau and the two brothers became reconciled. They did not join forces, however, and nothing further is said about Esau. The story in Genesis concentrates on Jacob and his family. He had twelve sons. His favourite was Joseph and he gave him a long robe with sleeves. (Some English translations have 'a coat of many colours', but this is a mistake.) This would be a special honour. It distinguished Joseph from his brothers and suggested that he need not work, for such a robe would be quite unsuitable for the kind of work they had to do. When he was seventeen years old Joseph had two dreams in which he appeared to be lord over the rest of the family, who bowed down to him. He foolishly told his father and his brothers about these dreams and his brothers hated him and decided to get rid of him.

There were two stories told of the way his brothers dealt with him and the editor of Genesis used both of them, combining them to form one connected narrative. In one story the brothers hated Joseph because of his dreams; they planned to kill him and fling his body into a pit— perhaps a dried-up well—pretending to their father that a wild animal had attacked him. Reuben, one of his brothers, saved him by suggesting that they should not kill him but simply put him into the pit; he intended to rescue him later on. Some Midianite traders who were passing noticed Joseph in the pit, hauled him up and took him to Egypt, where they sold him as a slave. Reuben returned to the pit and found it empty. The other story related that the brothers hated Joseph because of the robe their father had given him. They plotted to murder him but Judah, another brother, persuaded them not to. At his suggestion they handed him over instead to some Ismaelite traders who were passing, who took him to Egypt and sold him. The brothers dipped Joseph's robe in the blood of a goat and took it to Jacob as evidence that he had been killed. It is not difficult to separate the two traditions as they were put together in Genesis. The 'dream' story is in chapter 37, verses 5-11, 18-20, 21-22, 28 (first part), 29-30, 36. The 'robe' story is in verses 3-4, 12-18, 23, 26-27, 28 (second part), 31-35 and is concluded in 39.1.

In Egypt Joseph's fortunes were varied. The man to whom he was sold was Potiphar, an officer of the royal court, who had him put in prison on a false accusation. He was released when he showed that he could interpret dreams, particularly one which the Pharaoh had. He was able to foresee that a time of famine was coming. The life of Egypt depended on the Nile; if this river did not rise every year and water the land, it would be impossible for the crops to grow. Joseph warned the Pharaoh and advised him to store up corn in advance. Joseph was put in charge of the distribution of food during the period of shortage and rose to a position of great authority in the land.

The famine extended to Canaan; when Jacob heard that there was grain in Egypt, he sent some of his sons there to bargain for supplies. Joseph interviewed them, at first treating them roughly. When at last he made himself known to them, they were terrified, thinking that he would take his revenge for the harm they had done him; but he generously forgave them and invited the family to come to Egypt. So Jacob and his clan migrated there. Many of the Hebrew tribesmen no doubt remained in Canaan but the writer of Genesis ignored them, for he was interested only in the family of Jacob and his descendants. They were now called Israelites or the sons of Israel.

One of the things that puzzle some people in these early stories in Genesis is the long life that some of the characters are said to have had. The flood-myth states that Noah was 950 years old when he died. In the accounts of the patriarchs Abraham is credited with 175 years and Isaac 180. These numbers are quite unreliable. No records were kept of the date of a man's birth and death and numbers were used in a very vague fashion; 'forty years' meant simply a long time, while a very short time was called 'three days'. Before they were written down, the stories were repeated again and again and story-tellers have always liked to impress their hearers by adding wonderful details. So the ages of the heroes got exaggerated; this often happened in the traditions of many ancient people.

During this period the patriarch of the tribe was not only the chieftain but also acted as priest of the tribal God. It was his duty to approach the God on behalf of the tribe when they wished for his help or when they felt that they had offended against his laws. The God of each tribe had a special, personal name, to distinguish him from others. The name of the Hebrew God consisted of four letters— YHWH. The Jews considered this such a sacred name that they never used it in speaking but always substituted another word which means 'the Lord'. So we cannot be certain how this was pronounced, for in the Hebrew language there are only consonants and the vowels are not written. The most probable pronunciation of the name is Yahweh. In the English Bible, wherever 'the LORD' appears, the Hebrew word is this name. The word Jehovah is sometimes used in English, but this is a mistake. It is a name made up from the consonants of Yahweh with the vowels of the word for 'Lord'.

Some of the stories about the patriarchs are often re-garded now as folk-lore rather than strict historical records of the activities of individuals. There is little doubt that Abraham, Isaac and Jacob existed but we cannot be sure that they actually did all the things which are related about them. Legends became attached to their names. The individual leaders sometimes seem to stand for the tribe as a whole or for different types of people. Abraham represents the father of the race, Lot the nomad who became a city-dweller, Esau the more primitive hunting folk, Jacob the stay-at-home settler and, after his name was changed to Israel, he stands for the better side of the character of the Hebrews. In spite of this folk-lore aspect, the stories do rest on early traditions and they give a life-like picture of the period between 2000 and 1500 B.C. The statements about customs and ideas have sometimes been confirmed by the discoveries of archaeologists. But the Hebrews preserved these stories not merely as a record of ancient history. There were probably many other traditions about the patriarchs, but these were selected in order to show how the early Hebrews de-pended on their God Yahweh and how he protected them. We can also see here how the Hebrews developed in their ideas and how the patriarchs were pioneers of their time— how Abraham was led to forsake the city with its perils and evils, how he rejected human sacrifice, how Jacob realised at Bethel that God was not confined to the territory of the tribe. In these ways the early Hebrews, although they shared many ideas and practices of the other Semitic nomads, were in advance of other peoples in the ancient world.

PASSAGES REFERRED TO IN THIS CHAPTER:

Abraham migrates to Canaan: *Genesis* 12.1 to 12.9.

Abraham and Lot separate: *Genesis* 13.2 to 13.13.
Abraham's offering of Isaac: *Genesis* 22.1 to 22.14.
Jacob gets Esau's birthright: *Genesis* 25.27 to 25.34.
Jacob gets his father's blessing: *Genesis* 27.1 to 27.45.
Jacob's experience at Bethel: *Genesis* 28.10 to 28.22.
Jacob's experience at the brook Jabbok: *Genesis* 32.22 to 32.31.
Joseph is taken to Egypt: *Genesis* 37.1 to 37.36.
Jacob's sons go to Egypt for grain: *Genesis* 42.1 to 42.17.
Jacob and his family settle in Egypt: *Genesis* 47.1 to 47.6.

CHAPTER

3

The Exodus from Egypt

The book of Genesis ends with the death of Joseph in
Egypt. The next two or three centuries are passed over
in silence. During that time the Hebrews increased in
numbers and more tribesmen from Canaan probably
joined them. They formed a community of settlers in the
district known as Goshen, between the Nile and the Gulf
of Suez. They probably carried on sheep farming and
cattle rearing which they had practised as nomads. But
they kept themselves separate from the other inhabitants,
for as Semites they were of a different race from the
Egyptians. A line of Semitic kings had occupied the throne
of the Pharaohs for a time and this may have been why
the Hebrews were allowed to stay. But there was a revolu-
tion and the Semitic kings were driven out and true
Egyptians took their place. The rulers began to be sus-
picious of these foreigners, the Hebrews, for they occupied
the land bordering on the eastern frontier—the direction
from which enemies could attack Egypt. The Old Testament says that a new Pharaoh arose who did not know
about Joseph; he was probably Rameses II, a young and
energetic ruler about whom much is told in Egyptian
records. He decided that the Hebrews would have to be
put to work in building fortifications and cities. A system

of forced labour was instituted and overseers were appointed who treated the workers harshly. But the Hebrews were a hardy folk and these stern measures failed to keep them under. So the Pharaoh finally issued an order that all male children of the Hebrews were to be put to death.

It was in this situation that Moses was born. His parents were Hebrews of the tribe of Levi (one of the sons of Jacob) and, after hiding him for three months, his mother set him adrift on the Nile in a cradle made from papyrus reeds, hoping that someone would rescue him. A royal princess found the baby there, took pity on him, took him home and brought him up as her own son. The Egyptians were a highly cultured people and Moses would receive a thorough education. He would learn about the geography and history of the land, their mathematics and science, astronomy and medicine, as well as the practices of magic and astrology and the Egyptian religion. But he knew that he was a Hebrew and not an Egyptian. One day when he was grown up he visited the place where the Hebrews were working and saw them being badly treated by an overseer. Moses knocked him down and killed him. Next day he again visited the Hebrew workers and tried to stop a quarrel between two of them. But they turned on him: 'Who set you up as a judge? Do you want to kill us, as you killed the Egyptian?' The news of what had happened reached the Pharaoh and Moses realised that Egypt was no safe place for him. He fled from the country, following the trade route eastwards to the Sinai peninsula. It was known then as the land of Midian. The inhabitants were of the same race as the Hebrews and Moses found a welcome among them and entered the service of Jethro, a chieftain and priest of the Midianite God. He married Jethro's daughter and no doubt thought that he was settled there for the rest of his life. But he was roused one day by an experience he had when he was looking after Jethro's flock on the side of a mountain called Horeb.

The account in the book of Exodus says that his attention was drawn to a 'flame' in a bush which was on fire. Some have suggested that the brilliant blossom of a tree or shrub seemed in the sunshine to be aflame; others think it was some electrical or volcanic activity. But in such a hot climate bushes in the desert easily catch fire. The appearance of a God was often described in those times as being like a fire or a powerful wind. When Moses approached a 'voice' told him that he was on holy ground. He was ordered to go to Egypt and demand the release of the Hebrews. He was to lead them out and bring them to that mountain to meet God. Moses protested that he was unfit for this task. He said that they would not listen to him and asked how he was to prove that God had commissioned him. How was he to tell the Hebrews which God had sent him to deliver them? What was his name?

The answer he received was : 'I am who I am'. He was to say to the Hebrews: 'I AM has sent me to you'. This is an explanation of the name Yahweh. The four consonants of this word are taken from the verb 'to be' in Hebrew. The name was probably meant to convey two ideas—first, that Yahweh was all-sufficient and the Hebrews could rely on him; second, that he was a God of action. The Semites were a very practical people; for them, real existence meant activity. If a man did not do anything he could not be said to be really alive. So the name of Yahweh—'I am'—meant that he was acting on behalf of his people, that he would support them and be their leader.

It may seem strange to us that here, as in many other parts of the Old Testament, a conversation between God and a man seems to be reported, as if two people were talking together. This is not our way of describing a man's experience of guidance from God, but ancient writers, especially in the east, often put it in this dramatic form.

We can appreciate this better when we remember that such stories were told by word of mouth before they were eventually written down and this dramatic dialogue form would make a great impression on the hearers and help them to remember the account. Mount Horeb was probably a place which was considered sacred by the Midianites and some people think that they worshipped Yahweh as their God. What Moses realised here was that this was the same God as the one whom his Hebrew ancestors had worshipped and he was to remind the Hebrews of this when he returned to Egypt to deliver them from their state of slavery.

Moses then left Jethro his father-in-law and, accompanied by his brother Aaron, returned to Egypt. He asked the Pharaoh if he might lead the Hebrews eastwards into the desert for a short distance—'a three days journey', he said—so that they might make a sacrifice to their God. The Pharaoh thought this was a trick; he naturally thought that once they got away they would not return or they might collect a force of allies and attack Egypt. Their employers were also probably unwilling to lose such a source of cheap labour. Instead of granting permission, the Pharaoh decreed longer hours and harder tasks for the Hebrew workers.

A long struggle followed between Moses and Aaron and the Pharaoh, in which they tried to convince the Egyptian ruler of the power of their God. They performed various tricks, but these were also reproduced by the magicians at the royal court. The lot of the Hebrews got harder. The story of this period in the Old Testament is confused and there seems to be much repetition. This is because the writers have put together a number of accounts which did not always agree. Eventually a series of disasters or 'plagues' struck the people of Egypt. First the water of the Nile became fouled. The account says that it was turned into blood. Perhaps some impurity further up the river caused some discolouration of the water. The Nile still becomes a dirty red colour in June or July. The fish—a staple food of the Egyptians—died in the river. Then followed a plague of frogs, which had probably left the Nile to invade the land. Mosquitoes and flies came next, as one might expect. These of course brought disease, which at first affected the cattle. Then boils broke out on both animals and men. A violent hail-storm devastated the crops and finally there was an invasion by locusts. This can still be a great disaster in many eastern countries and a cloud of locusts descending on the fields can destroy within an hour the labour of months or years.

All these calamities happen at times in Egypt. The fact that they came one after the other within a short period was taken by the Hebrews as evidence that Yahweh was supporting them. They decided that he could wield his power even over Egypt, whose gods could not protect their own land. The Pharaoh seems to have thought much the same, for he summoned Moses and told him to take his troublesome people away. The event which decided him was an epidemic of some kind which struck particu-larly at the men among the Egyptians. The Old Testa-ment writer says that the first-born of each family was killed. The Hebrews were not affected. They were probably more healthy than the Egyptians in the big cities and not so liable to succumb to disease.

Moses had made full preparations for the departure of the Israelites and had instructed them to have a final meal. This was to be taken standing, in readiness for flight, and consisted of a lamb eaten with bitter vegetables and unleavened bread—made without using yeast. There would be no time for the usual careful preparations. Blood from the lamb had to be smeared on the doors of their houses. The intention in this was probably to keep off evil spirits while they were having their meal. The later

29

Hebrews said that the epidemic which afflicted the Egyptians was brought about by Yahweh, who 'passed over' the houses of the Israelites when he saw the blood. So this meal got the name of Passover.

Then Moses collected the tribes and led them eastwards from Egypt. It was too dangerous to follow the usual route along the coast towards Canaan, for that was strongly fortified by the Egyptians. So they proceeded towards the Sinai peninsula by a route further south, to the north of the Gulf of Suez (see map on p. 33). But in the meantime the Pharaoh had changed his mind about letting these useful slaves escape. He sent after them a force of cavalry and chariots. The Hebrews were terrified at this sudden threat, thinking they were caught between the sea in front of them and their enemies behind. But Moses knew the geography of the district better than they did. He told them not to fear and led them forward. They got safely across into Sinai but their Egyptian pursuers did not.

This event is generally called the crossing of the Red Sea but this phrase is incorrect and misleading. 'Red Sea' is a mistranslation of a Hebrew phrase which means 'sea of reeds'. This was an old name for the Gulf of Suez. The Red Sea is 250 miles further south and it would have been senseless as well as dangerous for Moses to have led his large company there, when there was a route in front of them due east from the land of Goshen. The Suez Canal now links the Gulf of Suez with the Bitter Lakes north of it and runs on to the Mediterranean coast. But before this was constructed a hundred years ago, the land between the water was comparatively dry, although no doubt rather marshy. The Israelites took a route either between the lakes or between the northern tip of the Gulf and the lakes. Barefoot and lightly clad, with few possessions, they got across quite safely. But the Egyptians on their horses and in heavy chariots got stuck and could not follow them. If the crossing was at the north of the Gulf of Suez, the incoming tide may have caught them as well.

Two narratives were told about this event, which is generally referred to as the exodus (a word meaning 'departure'). The older account told of a strong east wind which blew during the night. Coming from the dry area of the desert, it would harden the marshy ground. This story goes on to say that the wheels of the Egyptian chariots got clogged, so that they could not make any progress. Those which were not stuck in the mud turned back and gave up the pursuit. The other version said that Moses stretched out his arm and the water was divided, so that there was a 'wall of water' on both sides of the Hebrews. When they had got across, the water returned and the Egyptians were drowned. This is a later story, written to emphasise the marvel of the deliverance. In such accounts anything which appeared to be wonderful or miraculous tended to be exaggerated. The story in the book of Exodus contains both these versions; the editor put them both down without trying to make them agree.

The Israelites saw in their deliverance the work of Yahweh. Once more, they said, he had proved that he was stronger than the Egyptian gods. The event made a great and lasting impression on the Hebrew people. They considered that it marked the beginning of their life as a nation and the Passover meal which they had held before leaving Egypt became an annual celebration. It is still observed by Jews all over the world, in March or April, in commemoration of the exodus from Egypt.

The Hebrews now became nomads again, in the Sinai peninsula. The district, although generally called the 'wilderness of Sinai', was not complete desert. It was more like bare moorland or steppe country. Flocks and herds could find some pasture but food for men was not so easy. The Israelites would camp at various spots but never settled for a long time. Their destination was Canaan, but the people who had left Egypt were in no fit state to invade another country. They still had a slave mentality, which was shown in the way they constantly grumbled at Moses. When they found that food was short, they complained and declared they would rather go back to Egypt than suffer there; at least they had had enough to eat. A condition of slavery was better than death in the wilderness. But Moses was resourceful. He appears to have had the gift of water-divining and on one occasion, possibly two, he was able to find a stream hidden behind the rocks. Once flocks of quails—a kind of partridge—which were migrating over the area settled near the camp, tired by their flight. The Israelites were able to swoop down on them and capture them for food. Another time they found in the mornings a white substance on the ground which was edible. They said it was 'bread from heaven' and called it manna. It may have been dropped by insects or it was some mushroom-like growth which quickly came up overnight. Some people think it was sap from trees like the tamarisk, which exudes a white substance. On these occasions Moses took the opportunity to rebuke them for their faithlessness, pointing out that Yahweh was looking after them, ungrateful though they were. They also had to struggle against other tribes, but they made an alliance with the Midianites when they arrived at the district where Jethro lived.

Moses had the task not only of seeing to their material needs such as food but also of keeping them loyal to Yahweh. They had with them a large tent, which stood for God's presence among them, which was their place of worship. But it was not at all like a modern church, where a congregation can meet. Only priests were allowed inside the tabernacle (as this tent was called); it was surrounded by a large outer court where the people or their leaders could assemble. The inner part of the

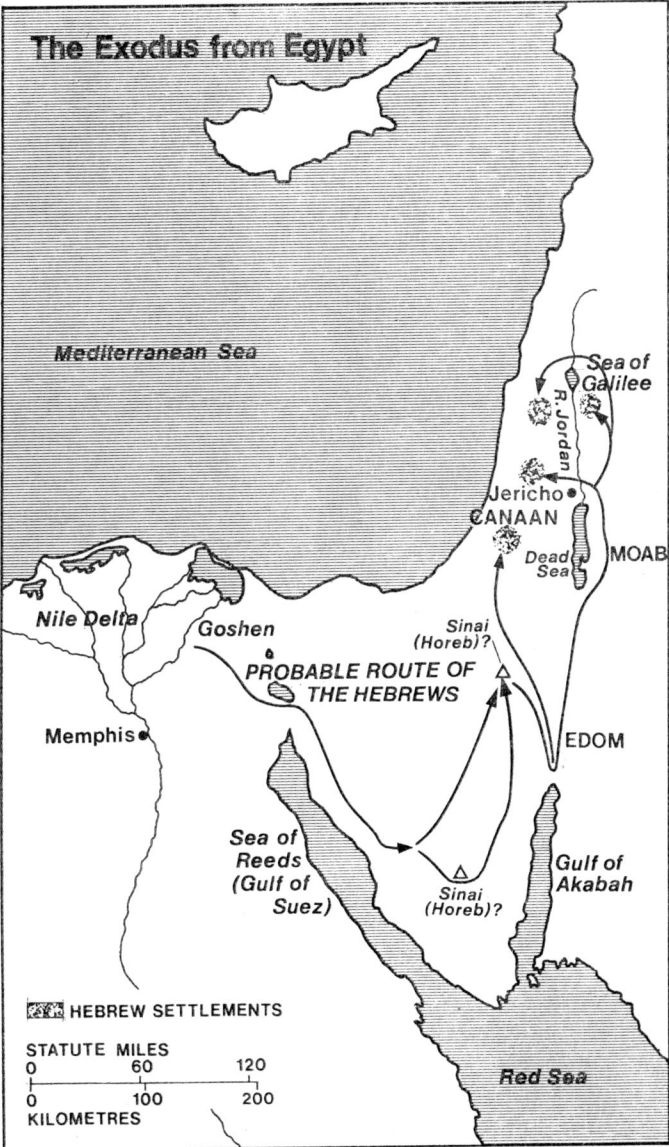

The Exodus from Egypt

Mediterranean Sea

Sea of Galilee

R. Jordan

Jericho
CANAAN

Dead Sea

MOAB

Nile Delta

Goshen

Sinai (Horeb)?

PROBABLE ROUTE OF THE HEBREWS

Memphis

EDOM

Sea of Reeds (Gulf of Suez)

Sinai (Horeb)?

Gulf of Akabah

HEBREW SETTLEMENTS

STATUTE MILES
0   60   120

0   100   200
KILOMETRES

Red Sea

tabernacle contained the 'Ark of the Covenant'—a wooden chest about $4\frac{1}{2}$ feet long and just over 2 feet broad and deep. This represented the presence of Yahweh and inside it were later placed tablets of stone on which were inscribed the laws of their society and their religion. The priests were the leaders of the community. They were the only men qualified to make sacrifices inside the tabernacle. They also sought to find out the will of God for the people. They did this by means of two sacred stones which gave them negative or positive answers to the question of what they should do in a particular situation. The priests also announced important events and gave the sign for beginning a battle by blasts on trumpets. They summoned the Israelites to an assembly in the same way—the tabernacle was sometimes called the 'tent of meeting'—and the leaders or 'elders' of the tribes, whom Moses had appointed, came there to hear some pronouncement from him or to discuss what they should do.

The tribes eventually arrived at Mount Sinai. This was another name for Horeb in the Midianite country, where Moses had received the call to lead the Hebrews from Egypt. It is not certain where this was. There is a mountain still called Sinai in the south of the peninsula and this may have been the place. But some think that Horeb was to the north-east of the peninsula, between the Gulf of Akaba and the Dead Sea. A graphic description is given in Exodus of what appears to have been volcanic activity, for the account tells of thunder and lightning, a thick cloud over the mountain, loud noises like a trumpet blast and the ground shaking. The Hebrew writer said that this meant Yahweh was 'descending on the mountain in fire'. The people had to keep at a distance, but Moses went up to meet God. The story is told again in the form of a conversation between Moses and Yahweh. Moses was given and instructed to take to the people the laws which we call the Ten Commandments. These laid down the fundamental rules for the community.

The first four commandments relate to the Hebrews' religion:

(1) They were to have only one God and no others. They were to be faithful only to Yahweh.

(2) They were not to make any images. Other nations had figures carved from stone or made of metal which represented their gods. The Hebrews worshipped an invisible God. They might be tempted to treat images as objects of worship, so they were forbidden to make any at all.

(3) The name of God was not to be used 'in vain' or in the wrong way, lightly or carelessly, but with due reverence. The Hebrews never even pronounced the name of Yahweh.

(4) They were to keep the last day of the week sacred, as a sabbath (a word which means 'rest'), when no work at all was to be done. This was a practice among other ancient peoples as well, but we do not know the origin of it. Two reasons are given in the Old Testament, for these ten commandments appear in two different places. The version in *Exodus* 20 says that God made the world in six days and rested on the seventh, so men must do the same. This refers to the creation-myth which is now in *Genesis* 1. But the Hebrews knew and adapted this Babylonian story about seven hundred years later than the time of Moses, so this reason could not have been given by him. The other account, in *Deuteronomy* 5, says that the Sabbath was to remind them that they had been slaves in Egypt and the day was to be observed in commemoration of their deliverance.

The last six commands are practical and moral, relating to conduct and the attitude towards other people. They were: Honour father and mother (5), do not kill or commit murder (6) or commit adultery (7) or steal (8) or give false evidence (9) or covet anything which belongs to someone else (10). The last one is remarkable in that it deals not with outward action but with the inner state of mind. It condemns the spirit of greed which might lead to stealing or killing. These old commands are worth examining today, to see how far they apply to us and our lives. We may not have much to do with the first four, which relate to the religious observances of the Jews, but the last six are the basis of a sound structure of society, in any age.

It is probable that the form of these commandments as we read them in the Old Testament comes from a later date, when the Hebrews had settled down as a nation, but the basis of the laws probably goes back to the time of the stay in the wilderness. They were in advance of the laws of other nations and religions of that day. One feature is that they were all regarded as religious regulations, even the last six, all said to have been given to Moses by Yahweh. The Hebrews considered that God was interested not only in the people's manner of worship and their beliefs but also in their social conduct. The practice of honouring one's parents, doing justice, refraining from evil deeds was all God's concern, as much part of their religion as worship and reverence towards him.

The Hebrews often fell below these high ideals of conduct and religious practice. They continued to grumble at Moses. They got dissatisfied with the idea of a God whom they could not see and, when Moses had been up the mountain for a long time, they turned to his brother Aaron and asked him to make an image for them. So he told them to hand him the jewelry that they had taken from the Egyptians and, melting this down, he made an image of gold in the form of a calf. The bull was a symbol of strength and this was probably intended to represent the power of Yahweh. 'Look', he said, 'there is your God who led you from Egypt.' The next day they held a special festival and made sacrifices before the bull-image, with singing and dancing, as was customary in religious celebrations. In the midst of this Moses came on the scene. For the second time he is reported to have lost his temper. He was so indignant that he broke the stone tablets on which he had written the laws, smashed the image and ground it down to powder. Aaron made feeble excuses, putting the blame on the people. Moses called on the tribe of Levi to put the ringleaders to death. The writer says that this was Yahweh's punishment of the people. This shows that they still thought of God as cruel and revengeful, as did other nations at that time.

We have little information on how long the Hebrews remained in the district of Sinai or what they did after leaving it. The book of Exodus has several chapters at this point which were put together later, on the terms of the covenant which Moses and the people made with Yahweh. Then there follows a book called Leviticus, which consists mainly of regulations for the priests and is of a much later date. It was written when the Israelites were settled in Canaan and had a temple at Jerusalem. The next book is called Numbers, because it mentions two occasions on which Moses counted the people or took a census, and is also mostly late; and after that comes Deuteronomy (a title which means 'second law'), containing a repetition of the earlier laws, with many others added. The Jews called these first five books in the Old Testament the 'books of Moses', because he was thought to have written them; but we know now that they consist of writings of many men at different periods, which were edited and arranged much later than Moses.

The Israelites are said to have been in the wilderness for forty years. This was the usual round number meaning a long time. This was necessary if they were to enter

Canaan, for the people who had left Egypt had to die out. They had a slave-mentality and they would not have been physically strong. Their children grew up used to a stern life in the open air and were more hardy. The Hebrews eventually stopped at Kadesh, some fifty miles south of Canaan, and from there Moses sent out twelve men as scouts into the country. They returned saying that it was a fertile land—'a land flowing with milk and honey' was the proverbial expression they used—and they brought back some grapes to show this. But they were frightened of the inhabitants. They had walled cities, which the Hebrew nomads had never seen before, and to the shorter men from the desert region they seemed like giants. Only two of the scouts, Joshua and Caleb, advised them to put their trust in Yahweh to help them to conquer the country.

The Hebrews then seem to have travelled to the country of Moab, on the eastern side of the Dead Sea. There Moses died; Aaron had died some time before. Moses himself never entered Canaan but climbed a mountain in Moab from which he could look across the Jordan valley and see the 'promised land'. He was ever afterwards revered as a great leader. He was considered a man through whom God spoke—a prophet, priest and law-giver. He was regarded by the Jews as the founder of the covenant between their nation and God. He certainly did much to make the Hebrew tribes more like a nation, but this work was still far from complete at his death.

PASSAGES REFERRED TO IN THIS CHAPTER:

The Egyptians enslave the Hebrews: *Exodus* 1.8 to 1.13.
The birth and upbringing of Moses: *Exodus* 2.1 to 2.10.
Moses champions the Hebrews: *Exodus* 2.11 to 2.15.

Moses receives a call to rescue the Hebrews: *Exodus* 3.1 to 3.22.

The crossing of the 'sea of reeds': *Exodus* 14.5 to 14.29.

The 'song of Moses', to celebrate this: *Exodus* 15.1 to 15.12.

Moses brings the Israelites to Sinai: *Exodus* 19.16 to 19.25.

The ten commandments: *Exodus* 20.1 to 20.17.

Deuteronomy 5.6 to 5.21.

Aaron makes a golden image: *Exodus* 32.1 to 32.6 and 32.15 to 32.28.

The spies sent into Canaan: *Numbers* 3.1 to 3.3; 3.17 to 3.33 and 14.1 to 14.9.

Moses dies within sight of Canaan: *Deuteronomy* 34.

4

The Hebrews in Canaan

Before Moses died, he had appointed Joshua to be leader of the tribes. He was a much younger man and had the energy which Moses lacked. The Hebrews were now far better equipped to invade a country than their parents had been when they had left Egypt. They were stronger and more hardy and had learnt much from their struggles in the wilderness. They also had on the whole a firmer faith in their God and possessed the laws of Moses which should help them to maintain a high standard of conduct.

The inhabitants of the land to which they had come are generally known by the name of Canaanites but they consisted of a number of different tribes. The country had been under the control of Egypt for hundreds of years but the Egyptian power seems to have been weak at this period. There was nothing like a central government over the whole land. The people lived in scattered villages with a few walled towns. They were of the same race, the Semitic, but they were not united into a nation. There was inter-tribal rivalry and even wars; sometimes a group of tribes would make an alliance against a common enemy. Quite probably there were also Hebrews living in Canaan, for not all the Hebrews had gone to Egypt with

Jacob. The Canaanites would naturally resist the coming of fresh hordes of Hebrew nomads.

There are two accounts in the Old Testament of the Israelite invasion of Palestine (the name later given to Canaan) after the death of Moses. One describes a united campaign under the leadership of Joshua, in which all the tribes acted together to effect a swift conquest of the country. The other account, which is an earlier one and more likely to be correct, tells of three or four groups of tribes which acted independently, each trying to settle in a different area. One group, led by the tribe of Judah, settled in the southern part, between the Dead Sea and the Mediterranean coast. Another group crossed the Jordan just north of the Dead Sea and made for the hill country in the centre of the land. These were led by the tribe of Ephraim. A third group went further north, probably crossing the Jordan north of the lake of Galilee, while a fourth group remained east of the Jordan. These four groups seldom acted together; the common link between them was their loyalty to the same God, Yahweh. (See map, p. 33.)

Joshua was the leader of the second, Ephraim, group. He first got the people across the Jordan. There seems to have been a landslide or a fall of rock further up the river which held up the water and the Hebrews took advantage of this and passed over on comparatively dry ground. The same thing has happened on a number of occasions in more recent times. They then faced their first obstacle—the city of Jericho. If they were to make any further progress, they would have to take it. Jericho was a very ancient city which has been attacked many times in the course of its history. Archaeologists have discovered many Jerichos around or under the present city which still bears the same name. Its defences were not very strong and it was likely to fall fairly easily to a determined attack. The climate in the Jordan valley—more than a thousand feet below sea level—was hot and humid and this tended to make the inhabitants lazy and unable to resist a siege or an assault.

Joshua first sent scouts to find out the situation. They were received by a woman named Rahab, who had a house built into the city wall. When the authorities heard of the arrival of the spies, she hid them on the flat roof of her house and then let them down over the wall. They promised to safeguard her and her family when they attacked. The incident suggests that there were some within the city who would welcome the invaders. The Old Testament gives a vivid account of the methods the Hebrews employed. They first marched round the place for a week; this was probably intended to scare the inhabitants and to get them wondering what was coming next. Then, when the priests blew their trumpets, they marched straight up to the city and, the writer says, 'the walls collapsed'. Some people have suggested that there was an earth tremor which shook the foundations, but it is more likely that this is a graphic eastern way of saying that there was practically no opposition. The Hebrews said they were able to march in as if the walls were not there; perhaps Rabah and her associates had opened the gates to the invaders.

Joshua gave orders that the city was to be destroyed, with every living creature within it (except for Rahab and her household). He felt that, if he left it standing, the Hebrews might be tempted to stay in the unhealthy Jordan valley. Jericho was considered typical of many cities and represented a low standard of life and morals. Joshua knew that the Hebrews would be ruined if they settled there; they were to make for the hill country in the centre of the land. We consider that the destruction of Jericho and other cities was a cruel and savage action. It seems even more horrible that Joshua ordered this at the command of Yahweh. But we must not judge him by our Christian standards. The Hebrews' idea of God was still primitive. They thought: Yahweh has enabled us to take the city, which has stood in his way, so he would have us wipe it out. This was quite a common practice at that time.

For many years the different groups of Hebrews were trying to settle in Palestine. It was a difficult task. They could not conquer the land as a whole; in some places they overpowered the native inhabitants but at other times they had to submit to the rule of the Canaanites. In some districts there would be Israelite villages alongside of Canaanite strongholds. Some of the Canaanite tribes had 'kings'—not much more than tribal chieftains, but they had absolute power over the territory they ruled and constituted a more permanent form of government than the Hebrews had. The Israelites also suffered attacks from the peoples around the central area of Canaan— Ammonites on the eastern bank of the Jordan, Moabites from the Dead Sea district, Amalekites in the south and Midianites who occasionally came up from the desert and attacked the settlements or raided the corn fields. In the centre of the part where the tribe of Judah settled, the Jebusites occupied a stronghold among the hills, called Jerusalem. A danger which threatened all the people of Canaan came from the Philistines, who had settled along the south-west coast. These were not Semites but Europeans who had come across the sea, perhaps from Crete. They were more advanced in civilisation than the tribesmen and had more formidable weapons—iron spears and chariots. They built cities along the coast, one of which still keeps its old Philistine name of Gaza.

In their desperate situation the Hebrews were helped at various times by leaders who are generally called 'judges'. This is a misleading translation of the Hebrew word for them, which really means saviours or deliverers. In a Hebrew district which was being attacked by

43

Canaanites—or was even ruled by them—a local leader would rouse the people to throw off their oppressors. He would issue a call to arms, collect the men of the district and attack the Canaanites. These 'judges' often succeeded in freeing a group of tribes for a time but they did not set themselves up as permanent rulers and guerrilla warfare would continue between the rival peoples. Many of these men were religious champions as well as military leaders, calling the Hebrews to be faithful to Yahweh. Each Canaanite tribe had its own god, which was called a baal —a word meaning 'lord'. The baal was considered to be the real ruler of the particular locality. He gave the people prosperity and helped them to grow their crops and all the people living in the area were expected to acknowledge him. The Hebrews were sometimes in danger of thinking of their God in this way—as just a local baal. Some of them tried to combine the worship of Yahweh with reverence for the Canaanite baal as well. Many of the 'judges' protested against this. One of them, Gideon, started a revolt against the Midianites, who were oppressing his tribe at the time, by destroying an altar and an image of their goddess. He then made a sacrifice to Yahweh, before attacking the enemy. He weeded out all unwilling supporters and with a small force routed the Midianites by a trick. The Hebrews scared the enemy by making a great commotion in the night and putting them in confusion. The war cry of the Israelites was: 'A sword for the Lord and for Gideon!', for they thought of Yahweh as a leader in war, fighting with them.

One of these champions was a woman named Deborah. When Canaanite kings in the north had oppressed the Hebrews for many years, she called on a man, Barak, to collect an army. They enticed the Canaanite forces into the valley of the river Kishon, which flows out at the foot of mount Carmel, and when the rain came and the river rose the Canaanites were caught in the flood and were annihilated by the Hebrews. Sisera, the Canaanite captain, fled from the battle and came to the encampment of the Kenites, who were considered friendly to his people. He asked Jael, the wife of their chieftain, for shelter. She invited him in, gave him food and drink and assured him that he was safe. But when he was sleeping soundly she assassinated him by driving a tent-peg into his brain. This treacherous act is told twice in the book of Judges—first in a prose account and then in a poem called the Song of Deborah, which is one of the oldest pieces of writing in the Bible. It praises Jael and ends with the fierce refrain: 'So perish all thine enemies, Oh Yahweh; but let all who love thee be like the sun rising in strength.' This story well illustrates the savage nature of the times, as well as the imperfect conception of God which the Hebrews still had.

One of the best known of these champions is Samson, the traditional strong man of the Hebrews. He was not a typical 'judge' or deliverer at all. He was not a national or even a tribal leader but worked on his own—a self-centred, savage figure. He fought the Philistines, mostly for his personal glory, and seems to have had little or no religious feelings or principles. He was eventually betrayed into the hands of the Philistines by a woman, Delilah, and made a prisoner. When they were holding a celebration in honour of their god, his captors brought him out to show him to the crowds at the temple at Gaza. But his strength returned and he pulled down the building, killing himself along with many Philistines.

This period of chaos and general disorder in Canaan lasted for 150 to 200 years. Some Hebrew tribes settled down among the Canaanites, while others continued to fight and occasionally were even at war among themselves. The final disaster came when the Philistines captured the ark of the covenant. This was kept at Shiloh, a city in the south, in the charge of the priest Eli at the tabernacle. The Hebrews, after being defeated by the Philistines, had the idea of taking the Ark with them into battle. They thought that Yahweh would want to protect this sacred object and so they would be sure to win. When the Philistines heard what they were doing, it spurred them on to greater efforts, with the result that the Hebrews were defeated more heavily than before and the Philistines even captured the Ark. There is a dramatic account in the Old Testament of the way the news was brought to Shiloh, where Eli was sitting by the wall at the entrance to the town, waiting for a report from the battle. When he heard that the Israelites had been beaten, had suffered heavy losses, that his two sons were dead and, above all, that the Ark had been captured, the shock made the old man fall from his seat and killed him. In the meantime the Ark had been taken to Philistine territory. But various diseases broke out among them, which they put down to the influence of the Hebrew God. So they decided that the Ark was too dangerous an object to keep and they returned it to Hebrew territory.

After Eli the leading man at Shiloh was Samuel. As a small child he had been dedicated to God by his mother and had been brought up by Eli at the tabernacle. There is a story about an experience of his as a child which is a contrast to the warlike activities of the judges. He is said to have heard a voice at night calling him. He thought it was Eli and went to ask what he wanted, but the priest told him it was the voice of Yahweh. He was to reply: 'Speak, Lord, for thy servant hears'. Then Samuel was instructed to warn Eli about the conduct of his sons and his own slackness, for they were quite unworthy to follow in their father's place as priest.

After the death of Eli the leaders of the Hebrew tribes in the south came to Samuel and told him they wanted a king to reign over them. They realised the need for some regular system of law and order. The writer of the book of Judges well summarises the state of the country in his closing words: 'In those days there was no king in Israel and every man did what was right in his own eyes'. The Hebrews thought that if the tribes could be united under one ruler they would stand more chance of defeating their enemies and becoming a nation. There are two versions of Samuel's response to this request. One account says that it displeased him and he told them that in wanting to have a king like other peoples they were rejecting Yahweh, who was their true king. He warned them what a monarchy would mean—that they would have to pay taxes and would complain about the king's oppression, that he would take their young men to work and fight for him. The Hebrew kings did indeed often turn out to be like this and this account was put down later, because the writer thought that the demand for a king was a mistake. There are other stories, which are more likely to be accurate, which suggest that Samuel was willing to find a king for them and that Yahweh himself prompted him to look out for a man who would lead them.

The one whom Samuel chose was a young man named Saul. He was the son of a landowner, Kish, of the tribe of Benjamin in the south. When some asses had strayed from his father's farm, Saul set out with a servant to look for them. The two men wandered a long way and when they approached the city where Samuel lived the servant suggested that they should ask him for his advice. He referred to Samuel as a 'man of God' and as a 'seer'. This meant a man who had special insight; he could see further than others into the nature of a situation or the character of people and was thought to be in touch with God. Samuel had been thinking over the matter of the kingship and the Old Testament writer says that God had previously warned him that he would meet a man from Benjamin. When he saw Saul he recognised him as a

47

suitable person; the account says God told him: 'Here is the man whom I spoke to you about'. Samuel told Saul he need not worry about the asses and suddenly addressed him with the words: 'Who is it that all Israel is looking for? Is it not you and your father's family?' Samuel then gave Saul a special seat of honour at a religious festival which he was conducting. Next day, when Saul was about to return home, Samuel took him aside and privately anointed him. This was an ancient practice—to appoint a man as a priest or a king by putting oil on his head. It is still carried on today in several countries when a monarch is crowned.

After leaving Samuel, Saul met a company of prophets. The word prophet does not really mean someone who tells the future but a man who speaks forth on behalf of his God. Most ancient religions had such prophets and they are still to be found in some places in the Middle East. They generally lived together in a community and used to travel about the country in groups, urging the people to be faithful to their God or sometimes stirring them up against their enemies. So great was their enthusiasm that they often got into a state of trance called ecstasy. Their excited behaviour was taken to show that they were under a divine influence. The company of the prophets of Yahweh whom Saul met were in this state, playing musical instruments and shouting their message or 'prophesying' as they came down from a hill where a religious ceremony had been held. Saul caught the infection of their ecstasy and 'prophesied' with them, uttering the same excited cries as they were making. When people who knew him heard about this, they were surprised, for they did not think much of these wild prophets. 'Is Saul also among the prophets?' they remarked—a phrase which is still used as a proverb when someone is found in quite unexpected company. Saul eventually arrived home and when his uncle asked him what had happened he modestly said nothing about Samuel's promise of a kingship.

Saul continued working on his father's farm but he soon found an opportunity to prove himself a leader. News was brought that some Ammonites had attacked the Hebrew town of Jabesh-Gilead which was east of the Jordan. They had laid down barbarous terms of surrender —that they would put out the right eye of every man. Instead of merely lamenting, as other people were doing on hearing the news, Saul immediately sent to the tribes around and summoned them to help. He collected an army, broke through the Ammonite force and relieved the besieged town. This brought him to the notice of the Hebrew leaders and led them to make him king. Another account tells of a meeting of the tribes which was called by Samuel. He drew lots and selected the tribe of Benjamin, then the family of Kish and finally Saul himself. He was acclaimed king with a shout of 'Long live the king!'. In some versions of the Bible this is translated as 'God save the king'.

PASSAGES REFERRED TO IN THIS CHAPTER:

Joshua in command of the Hebrew tribes: *Joshua* 1.1 to 1.9.

The capture of Jericho: *Joshua* 6.8 to 6.21.

The defeat of Sisera and his murder by Jael: *Judges* 4.12 to 4.22.

Another account (in poetry) of this: *Judges* 5.24 to 5.31.

The death of Samson at Gaza: *Judges* 16.23 to 16.30.

Samuel the boy hears the voice of Yahweh: 1 *Samuel* 3.1 to 3.18.

The Philistines capture the Ark and the news is brought to Eli: 1 *Samuel* 4.1 to 4.18.

The Hebrews ask Samuel for a king: 1 *Samuel* 8.4 to 8.22.

Samuel meets Saul and anoints him: 1 *Samuel* 9 and 10.1
to 10.16.

Saul rescues the people of Jabesh-Gilead: 1 *Samuel* 11.1 to
11.11.

Saul is chosen as king by lot: 1 *Samuel* 10.17 to 10.24.

5

The Heberw Monarchy

Saul had many tasks to face when he became king. His position was a very difficult one for, as the first king of the country, he had to be a pioneer, without help from any previous experience or example of former kings. His capital was in the hill country in the middle of Canaan, but he had little chance to establish any settled form of government. He seems to have had little support from the tribes in the north. He had to conduct a long war against the Philistines, as well as ward off attacks from other nations around. His son Jonathan achieved several successes, but fighting continued for the whole of Saul's reign of twenty years or more.

Unfortunately Saul soon quarrelled with Samuel. On one occasion, when he wished to proceed to battle, he grew tired of waiting for Samuel to arrive, as the priest was to offer a sacrifice, so Saul performed the ceremony himself. When Samuel came he was very angry. Another time the king disobeyed Samuel's instructions to destroy completely the property of the Amalekites taken in battle and to kill their king. In this quarrel between the two men there were probably faults on both sides. Saul was impetuous and eager to assert his own power as king. Possibly Samuel was jealous of the position of the younger man and wanted still to exercise his old authority.

Samuel decided that Saul was unworthy. He thought that Yahweh had rejected Saul and looked round for someone to take his place. He visited the farm of a man named Jesse at Bethlehem in the south country and asked to see his sons. Not recognising in any of them a future king, he sent for the youngest, David, who was out with the sheep. Samuel privately anointed him as the future king of Israel.

Another trouble with Saul was a disturbance in his mind. He suffered from severe attacks of depression or melancholy which bordered at times on insanity. These made him irritable and unreliable—no fit condition for a king who had to command and make decisions. Today he would receive treatment from doctors and psychiatrists. In those times they said that an evil spirit had taken possession of him. His courtiers suggested that music might help him. There was no court musician but some-one said that he knew a youth at Bethlehem, David the son of Jesse, as one who was 'skilful in playing, a courageous man, a good fighter, careful in his speech, handsome and Yahweh is with him'. So David was sent for and he came to the court with a present for the king from his father and played before Saul on his lyre. Saul was refreshed and calmed by this; they said the evil spirit had been driven off.

There is another account of the introduction of David to Saul. The Philistines had a champion named Goliath, who came from a race of very tall men. He challenged any Israelite to single combat but nobody dared accept. David was visiting the camp with some food which he had brought for his three brothers who were in Saul's army, and heard Goliath. He said he would fight the man and was brought before Saul. He refused the armour which was offered him and killed the Philistines' champion with a stone from the sling that he used when guarding his father's sheep. Saul enquired who this youth was, for he had not seen him before, and appointed him to his court. The two stories were separate traditions of the way David came to the notice of Saul. The Old Testament editors put them down without attempting to reconcile them. In another book, however, there is a list of the 'mighty men of Saul' and among them is one called 'Elkanah, who killed Goliath of Gath'. It is possible that it was this man who actually killed the giant and the deed was later put down to the credit of David when he became a national hero.

Saul grew jealous of David because of his success and his popularity, for the people praised him more than they did the king. David became a friend of Jonathan, Saul's son, and Saul got the idea that David wanted to be king. When David played before Saul, the king in his frenzy threw his javelin at him. He even tried to kill Jonathan when he stood up for his friend. Eventually David had to flee from the court and was an outlaw for several years. He gathered around him hundreds of outlaws such as fugitives from justice, debtors who were evading their creditors and discontented men in general, and out of this band of desperate men he made a disciplined force. They roamed about the south country, sometimes raiding Canaanite tribes or the Philistines, trying always to keep out of Saul's way. The king trudged after David with his army, but he could never catch up with him. But David bore the king no grudge, for he was of a much better character than Saul, and on two occasions he even spared his life. Once he crept into the royal camp at night, right up to the place where Saul was sleeping. David's companion urged him to kill the king but David merely took away the royal spear and a jug of water, as a proof that he had been there. At another time David was in a cave when Saul entered. Once again David would not allow his men to kill the king, for he said he would not 'raise his hand against the Lord's anointed'. He simply cut off a corner of Saul's robe. David afterwards reproached him, saying that he had done no harm and yet Saul was after his life. The king appears to have been rather ashamed of himself, for he asked David to return. But David did not trust him and went back to his outlaw life.

The Philistines continued to harass the Israelites and advanced far into their territory. At Mount Gilboa, just south of the lake of Galilee, they thoroughly defeated Saul's army. Jonathan and two of his brothers were killed in the battle and the king fled in his chariot. He asked his armour-bearer to kill him but the man refused, so Saul committed suicide. The Philistines found the body and set it up as a trophy in honour of their gods who had given them the victory. The men of Jabesh-Gilead, the town which Saul had rescued years before, showed their remembrance of his deed. At great peril they went into the territory held by the Philistines, took the body back to their own town and cremated it with royal honours.

The news of the battle of Gilboa was brought to David by an Amalekite who claimed to have killed Saul himself. He thought that he would be rewarded for this but David told him he had committed a crime, for the king was still 'the Lord's anointed'. He had the man put to death. There follows then a poem lamenting the deaths of Saul and Jonathan, said to have been composed by David. It speaks of Saul as a mighty hero; the poet forbids the news to be proclaimed in the Philistine cities and curses Mount Gilboa where the tragedy happened. David especially mourns over the loss of Jonathan his friend and the poem concludes with a refrain: 'How are the mighty fallen!'

The people of Judah made David king (about 1010 B.C.), but the northern tribes favoured a son of Saul and there was civil war. It was not until seven and a half years had passed that David was acknowledged as ruler over the whole country. He achieved some notable successes. He eventually defeated the Philistines, so that they ceased to be a danger to Canaan and had to acknowledge the independence of Israel. One of his greatest achievements was to secure a worthy capital for his kingdom. The city of Jerusalem was a fortress which had been in the hands of the Jebusites ever since the Hebrew entry into Canaan. It was a very difficult place to attack, for it was situated on a number of hills in mountainous country, 2600 feet above sea level. David captured the city. It was a sound move to choose Jerusalem as his capital, for it was not in the territory of any particular tribe and none could be jealous. His headquarters previously had been at Hebron, in Judah. The sacred ark of the covenant was brought to Jerusalem and set up in the tabernacle, amid great rejoicing in which David himself took part. So Jerusalem became the religious as well as the political centre of his kingdom. He thought about building a temple there, as a more permanent place for sacrifices than the tabernacle. This would have been an important step, for it would have signified that the Israelites had put their nomadic past behind them and had really settled, like the nations around. A prophet, Nathan, advised against this and David left the project to his successor to carry out.

Later generations looked upon David as the ideal king of Israel. His successes were certainly impressive. He brought peace to the nation, not only keeping the Philistines off but also subduing the Canaanite tribes and bringing them under the rule of the Hebrews. He had not only a kingdom but an empire, for he extended his rule over foreign peoples outside Canaan itself. He conquered Edom in the south, the district around Damascus to the north-east and Moab and Ammon to the east of the Dead Sea and the Jordan. (See map on p. 58.) He showed considerable ability in ruling his own people. He consulted priests and prophets, and sacrifices and other ceremonies were regularly carried out at Jerusalem. By nature he seems to have been chivalrous and forgiving. At the beginning of his reign he made enquiries about any descendants of Saul and on finding a son of Jonathan who was lame he gave him a home in his royal palace. We do not hear anything more about his musical achievements, after his early performance before Saul, but later traditions spoke of him as a poet. The book of Psalms had his name attached to it, although this collection of hymns and poems was finally put together several centuries after David's time and many of them deal with situations about which he knew nothing.

Not all his deeds were praiseworthy; some of them simply reflected the outlook of an eastern monarch of the time. Some tribesmen had been wronged by Saul and he allowed them to put to death some of Saul's sons. He sometimes practised deceit. One of the blots on his character was the way in which he got his favourite wife. Monogamy was not practised at this time, especially by nobles and rulers, and David married several women, the first of whom was Saul's daughter. He became attracted by Bathsheba, the wife of a captain in his army named Uriah. This man was not a Hebrew but a Hittite, from people who came originally from the district north of Palestine and from Asia Minor. David ordered his general Joab to see that Uriah was put in the front line when they attacked an Ammonite city; then his comrades were to fall back and leave him to be killed by the enemy. When Joab reported that Uriah was dead, David took Bathsheba into his harem. In many eastern countries at the time David's action would be regarded as quite normal, for it was considered that a monarch could take any property of his subjects if he wanted it. But this story is different in two ways—someone denounced David for what he had done and the king repented.

The Old Testament writer says that David's action displeased Yahweh and he sent Nathan the prophet to him. Nathan told David an imaginary story—a rich man, with plenty of possessions, wanted to entertain a guest and had seized the only lamb of a poor neighbour. David was indignant at this injustice and act of tyranny. Then Nathan turned to him with the blunt words: 'You are the man!' He denounced David in the name of Yahweh, saying that he had broken his commandments in murdering Uriah and taking his wife. David did not order Nathan off to execution, as some kings would have done. He was ashamed of himself and said: 'I have sinned against Yahweh'. This account shows that the Hebrews had a higher notion of God than other peoples of the time. The gods of other nations had little or no concern about the moral lives of their worshippers but Yahweh was interested not only in their religion but in their everyday conduct.

In spite of David's successes there seems to have been discontent in the country. There was a rebellion led by one of his own sons, Absalom. This young man, who seems to have been spoilt by his father, tried to win the favour of the people. When men came to Jerusalem to ask David to settle their disputes—for the king acted as a judge as well as a monarch—Absalom would meet them and decide in their favour. 'If I were king', he would say, 'things would be different.' His influence among the people increased and he finally raised a revolt against his father. This was so successful at first that David had to leave Jerusalem, which was captured by the rebels. But the revolt was crushed by Joab and Absalom was killed while fleeing from the battlefield. There is a graphic account of the way in which the news was brought to David. When he heard of the death of his son he could only utter cries of sorrow: 'O my son Absalom. If only I had died instead of you!'

David had a long reign and lived to an old age. When

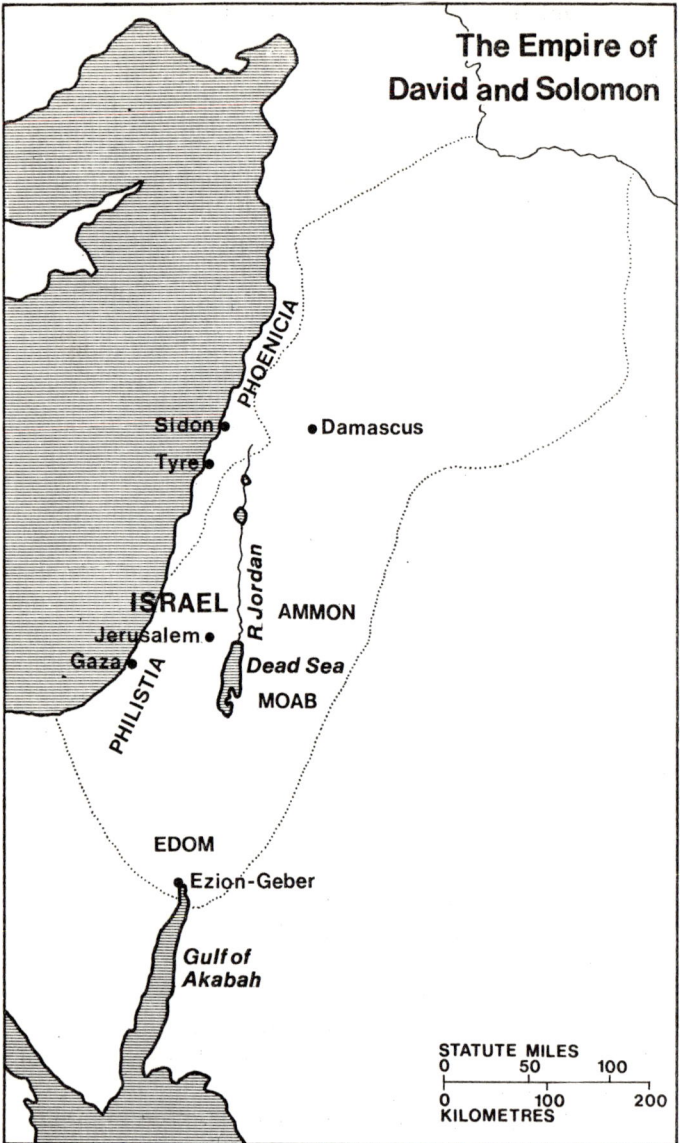

The Empire of
David and Solomon

PHOENICIA

Sidon

Tyre

• Damascus

R Jordan

ISRAEL

AMMON

Jerusalem

Gaza

Dead Sea

PHILISTIA

MOAB

EDOM

Ezion-Geber

*Gulf of
Akabah*

STATUTE MILES
0   50   100
0   100   200
KILOMETRES

he was too feeble to rule and evidently had not long to live, there was rivalry between two sons who wished to succeed him. One of them, Adonijah, was supported by Joab but the other, Solomon, who was the son of Bathsheba, was favoured by his mother and also had the backing of the prophet Nathan and the priest Zadok. These forestalled Adonijah and Joab and got Solomon proclaimed as king even before David was dead. He thus came to the throne as a result of a court intrigue.

Under Solomon the Hebrew kingdom attained its largest extent and its greatest magnificence. His influence is said to have extended from the Mediterranean coast to the Euphrates on the east and from the north of Palestine to the border of Egypt on the south-west. Neighbouring peoples paid taxes to him, acknowledging his overlordship, and he made a commercial treaty with the king of Tyre. This was the capital city of Phoenicia, an independent kingdom on the north-west coast of Palestine. The Phoenicians were an ancient seafaring people who for hundreds of years were powerful in the Mediterranean area by virtue of their trade and colonies. They established these on Malta and at Carthage in north Africa and in Spain. They traded even with Britain, purchasing tin from the mines in Cornwall. Solomon agreed that Israel should supply their king Hiram with corn and oil in return for a Phoenician labour force for his building schemes. Solomon also made treaties with other neighbouring nations and often confirmed the political or commercial arrangements by marriages with foreign princesses, including a daughter of the Pharaoh of Egypt. As they controlled Edom in the south the Hebrews had a port at the head of the Gulf of Akaba—the eastern arm of the Red Sea. Through this port they traded down the Red Sea with Africa and Arabia and probably even India.

Solomon was determined to make Jerusalem a worthy

capital of his empire. He had a great royal palace built.
with accommodation for all his officials and his haremf
An eastern king was expected to have a large number o,
wives, although the total attributed to Solomon in the
Old Testament is no doubt exaggerated. The building of
the royal palace took thirteen years. He also erected the
temple which David had contemplated. This was a
splendid construction. The temple building itself was
quite small—about thirty yards by ten. This was quite
sufficient, for it was entered only by priests and was not a
place for a congregation to worship like a modern church.
The innermost part of the temple was called the Holy of
Holies—the most holy place of all. This was thought of
as the abode of Yahweh himself. It was a cube in shape,
was in darkness and completely empty except for the
Ark of the Covenant, which was guarded by two huge
winged figures, made of wood covered with gold, called
cherubim. The other part of the building was called the
Holy Place. At the sides of the temple there were rooms
where priests and other officials lived. The temple building
was surrounded by a large courtyard, where there were
altars on which offerings were made and the bodies of
animals were burnt in sacrifice. There was finally a great
court which surrounded the whole area of the temple and
the royal buildings, in which people assembled when they
came on pilgrimage to Jerusalem.

In these ways Solomon gave Israel a great name
among the nations of the Middle East. The rival empires
of Assyria to the east and Egypt to the south-west were
both weak at this time, so Solomon was able to maintain
his power without interference. His wealth and magnificence made other peoples eager to trade with him and
even willing to acknowledge him as overlord. 'Solomon
in all his glory' is a phrase which has become proverbial.
He reigned as a great eastern monarch, over a country
that appeared to be thriving and prosperous, with a

splendid capital and luxurious royal court—a great contrast to the simplicity of the first king Saul and even to conditions in the time of David.

Solomon's personal character is not so easy to assess. He was evidently an able administrator and awake to the opportunities of his position. Later ages regarded him as a very wise man and a story is told how he was visited by Yahweh shortly after becoming king and was asked what gift he would choose for himself. He asked for 'a wise and understanding mind', to be able to govern justly. 'Wisdom' in the east meant the ability to judge and also to express general truths in short, pithy statements called proverbs. All such 'wisdom' came to be put down to the credit of Solomon, in the same way as poetry was attributed to David. The book of Proverbs in the Old Testament was not written by Solomon but is a collection of much later date. There is a story also that the queen of Sheba— an Arab monarch from the country we now know as Saudi Arabia—came to Jerusalem to test his wisdom. When she saw the wonders of his court she exclaimed in wonder and admiration and the two countries made a trade treaty.

But there was another side to Solomon's reign and character. He harshly suppressed the attempt of his half-brother Adonijah to gain the throne and had him put to death together with Joab, who had served David so faithfully as general of his army. Later Hebrew writers condemned him for his marriages with foreign wives. He probably considered these a clever political move, ensuring friendship with other nations. But when these women came to live in Israel they wanted still to practise their own religion; they could not be expected to worship the Hebrew Yahweh. Solomon made provision for them and in addition to the temple of Yahweh he had shrines and altars built in Jerusalem for the gods of the Phoenicians, Egyptians and other nations. He even made sacrifices to these gods himself. This caused much discontent among the loyal worshippers of Yahweh.

The most foolish and disastrous thing which Solomon did was in connection with the building of his palace and the temple. The people were heavily taxed to pay for these. He treated as slaves the non-Hebrew inhabitants, descendants of the Canaanites, made them work for him and instituted a system of forced labour for the Israelites. He had the country divided into twelve districts to supply food and work in turn for the operations at Jerusalem. But he made an exception in the case of his own tribe of Judah, for these people were not included in this scheme. This naturally caused bitterness and jealousy among the other tribes, especially those in the north who had no interest in what went on in Jerusalem and derived no benefit from the splendours of the capital. There was much discontent throughout the country and many were ready to rise in revolt against his harsh measures as soon as the opportunity offered.

Solomon's empire began to show weakness even during his reign. There was a rebellion in Edom, which meant that Israel lost its port on the Red Sea. At Damascus, to the north-east, a man named Rezon proclaimed himself as king and founded the independent kingdom of Syria. Within Israel itself a man of Ephraim named Jeroboam, who had been put in charge of the system of forced labour, planned a revolt but he had to flee to Egypt to take refuge from Solomon.

Solomon died about the year 930 B.C. and had appointed as his successor his son Rehoboam. The coronation of the new king was held at Shechem, in the centre of the country, not at Jerusalem; this may have been an attempt to gain the adherence of all the tribes and not only Judah. Representatives of the people came to Rehoboam and asked him to relieve them from the oppression that they had suffered under Solomon. 'Make our yoke lighter', they said, 'and we will serve you.' Rehoboam asked the advice first of the older men, the statesmen of his father's reign. Probably realising the justice of the people's demands, they advised him to make concessions. But the young king took the advice of companions of his own age, who told him to keep the people under by putting even heavier burdens on them. Solomon, they said, had 'chastised them with whips'; he should 'chastise them with scorpions'. When the people heard this they shouted that they had nothing to do with David's family and rejected the rule of his grandson. Rehoboam foolishly sent Adoram, who had been directing the forced labour, to put down the revolt. He was stoned to death and Rehoboam had to hurry in his chariot to get back to his fortress at Jerusalem.

Jeroboam had returned from Egypt on hearing of Solomon's death and the rebels now turned to him. He was proclaimed king over the central and northern tribes. His kingdom came to be known as Israel. Only the tribe of Judah in the south remained faithful to Solomon's son. The Hebrew kingdom, after lasting for about a hundred years, was split into two and was never again united.

PASSAGES REFERRED TO IN THIS CHAPTER:

The anointing of David by Samuel: 1 *Samuel* 16.1 to 16.13.
David plays before Saul: 1 *Samuel* 16.14 to 16.23.
The killing of Goliath: 1 *Samuel* 17.
David spares Saul's life: 1 *Samuel* 24 and 26.
The death of Saul: 1 *Samuel* 31.
David receives news of Saul's death: 2 *Samuel* 1.1 to 1.26.
The lament over Saul and Jonathan: 2 *Samuel* 1.17 to 1.27.
David gets Uriah killed: 2 *Samuel* 11.
Nathan denounces David: 2 *Samuel* 12.1 to 12.9.

David's grief at the death of Absalom: 2 *Samuel* 18.24 to
  18.34.
Solomon asks for wisdom: 1 *Kings* 3.5 to 3.15.
The queen of Sheba visits Solomon: 1 *Kings* 10.1 to 10.10.
Solomon acknowledges other gods: 1 *Kings* 11.1 to 11.8.
The revolt of the northern kingdom: 1 *Kings* 12.1 to 12.20.

6

The Two Hebrew Kingdoms

The empire which Solomon had possessed was now completely lost. The foreign nations which he had ruled had declared themselves independent. For two hundred years from the death of Solomon this area of the Middle East was split up into eight petty kingdoms, sometimes forming alliances but often fighting among themselves. (See map on p. 66.) All that was left to Solomon's son was the small kingdom of Judah, about the size of the county of Yorkshire.

The northern kingdom of Israel, ruled by Jeroboam, was in general more prosperous than the southern. The ground was more fertile and the country had the advantage of a sea coast. It was also on a trade route from Damascus in Syria, a great commercial centre. Judah was in country which was much more difficult to cultivate, with a range of mountains down the centre and a harsher climate. But it had the advantage of having the former capital in its territory and above all the temple, the central shrine of the Hebrews. Jeroboam realised the attraction of this for his own people and feared that they would continue to go to Jerusalem on pilgrimage. So he established two places in his kingdom where sacrifices could be offered to Yahweh. As he had no temple, he erected two

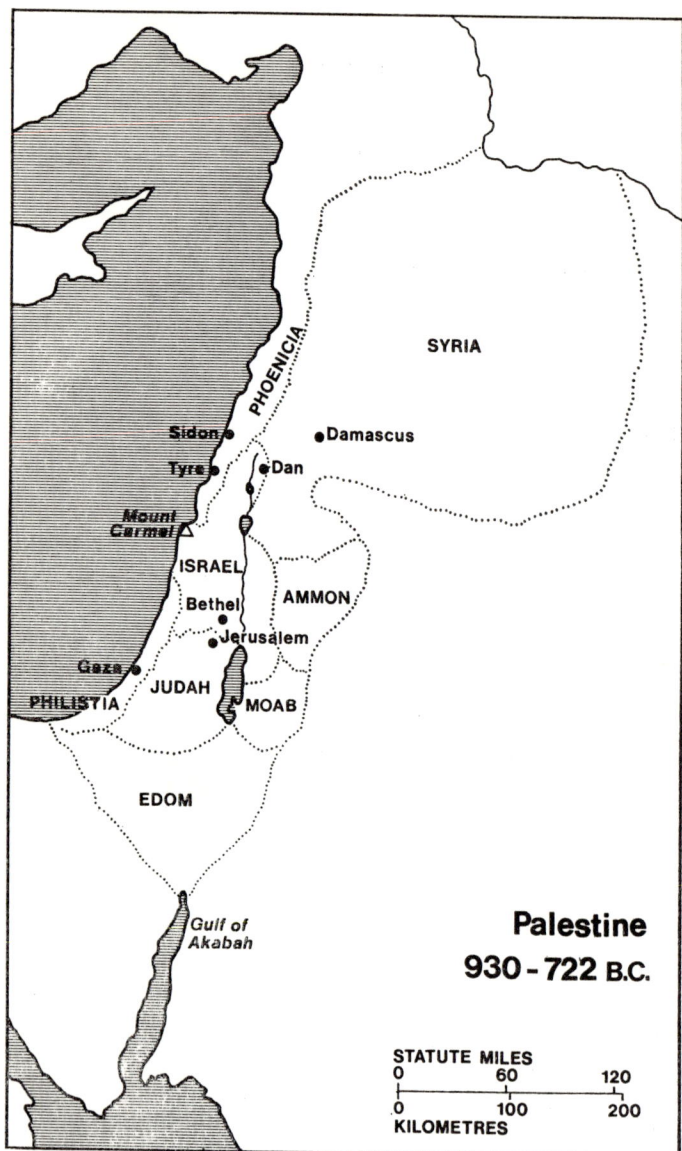

Palestine
930 - 722 B.C.

PHOENICIA

SYRIA

Sidon

Damascus

Tyre

Dan

Mount
Carmel

ISRAEL

Bethel

AMMON

Jerusalem

Gaza

JUDAH

MOAB

PHILISTIA

EDOM

Gulf of
Akabah

STATUTE MILES
0   60   120
0   100   200
KILOMETRES

images of bulls—one in the extreme north at Dan and the other at Bethel, only a few miles from the border of the southern kingdom of Judah. These were not intended as idols to be worshipped but represented the might of the Hebrew God. This action was regarded by the southerners as disloyalty and a great offence against Yahweh. The historical narratives in the Old Testament were compiled by men in Judah and they denounced the northern kings as those who 'caused Israel to sin after the fashion of Jeroboam'. We shall follow here the events in the northern kingdom and return to the southern one in the next period. Their fortunes were sometimes bound up together but they were quite often at war with each other.

Jeroboam seems to have been a capable ruler, although most of his reign was spent in strife with Judah. His son followed him but there was no regular line of succession. Many usurpers occupied the northern throne, often after the assassination of the previous king. One of the most important of Israel's rulers was Omri, about forty years after Jeroboam. He realised the need for a centre for his kingdom and built and fortified the city of Samaria as his capital. He ruled for a time the country of Moab, east of the Dead Sea. A large stone tablet was found in that district in 1868, called the Moabite Stone (now in the Louvre in Paris). It states that 'Omri oppressed Moab for many years' but their king threw off his rule with the help of Chemosh, the Moabite god. Omri's son, Ahab, warred against the kingdom of Syria but the two countries soon had to make a common front against the Assyrians, who had advanced from the Tigris-Euphrates valley. Assyrian forces severely defeated the armies of the two kingdoms, so that they had to pay tribute.

It was during this period that several prophets came into prominence in Israel. They were different from the company whom Saul met after he had left Samuel. Those men were religious fanatics who roamed the countryside in a state of excitement; similar prophets could be found in other nations at that time, with different religions. But now there appeared among the Hebrews another type of prophet—men who were calm, individual figures and stood apart from these excited companies. They had much to say about the way in which men should think of God and also the way in which they should act. Samuel, who was called a seer rather than a prophet, seems to have been one such, as was also Nathan, who denounced David when he had Uriah killed and took Bathsheba. In the reign of Ahab (about 860 B.C.) there were two other men who defied the king and refused to take the popular way because they felt that it was wrong and against the will of God.

One of these men was named Micaiah the son of Imlah. Ahab was in alliance with the king of Judah at that time and they were undecided whether to attack the Syrian fortress of Ramoth-Gilead. So Ahab called some of the ecstatic prophets before him and asked their advice. These all urged the kings to go forward and promised them victory. In their excitement they pranced about and shouted: 'Attack and win. Yahweh will give the city into your hands'. But when Micaiah was consulted he ignored this popular opinion and forecast disaster. 'I see Israel', he said, 'scattered about like sheep without a shepherd.' Ahab was furious and had him put in prison until he should return victorious. But in the battle which followed Ahab was killed.

The other individual prophet, about whom much more is known, was Elijah. Ahab married Jezebel, the daughter of the Phoenician king of Tyre. When she came to live at Samaria, she would not transfer her allegiance to Yahweh but continued her own religion. The Phoenicians worshipped the baal or lord of their land, called Melkart. To please her, Ahab had a temple built for Melkart in Samaria and priests came to sacrifice to the Phoenician

God. Jezebel also had her prophets introduced into Israel and she actually prevailed upon Ahab to persecute those who remained faithful to Yahweh. Many went over to the Phoenician God for fear of Jezebel and the Israelites were divided in their loyalties.

Elijah protested against this. Unlike Nathan, who had been at the king's court, Elijah was a man of the open country. He lived a solitary life like a hermit away from the towns, a wild figure dressed in skins. He would sometimes make a sudden appearance before the people or the king and, after uttering his message, return to the country. There had been a drought in the land for three years, which brought famine conditions. Ahab was one day searching for water for his horses when Elijah appeared in the road before him. Ahab greeted him as the 'troubler of Israel'. Elijah retorted that it was Ahab who had caused the trouble, because he had deserted Yahweh and followed the Phoenician baal. He issued a challenge to him. Let the prophets of Melkart come to Mount Carmel, to decide which was the God for Israel. This promontory on the coast, 1800 feet above the sea, was a place held sacred by both nations, and was an excellent spot for such a contest. From the top one could look north towards Phoenicia, to the east and south was Israel.

Four hundred priests and prophets of Melkart now gathered at Carmel and made a sacrifice to their god. Elijah demanded that they should call on him to show that he accepted their sacrifice by setting light to it. They went into a frenzy of excitement, dancing round the stone altar and crying out to Melkart. They even cut themselves with knives to show their devotion to their god or to call forth his pity. Elijah stood mocking them. 'Shout louder', he said, 'perhaps he has gone on a journey or perhaps he is asleep'—but nothing happened. When they had exhausted themselves, Elijah set up his sacrifice. He dug a trench round it and poured water into it and over the sacrifice. Then he spoke a calm prayer to Yahweh in great contrast to the despairing cries of the Phoenicians. Then 'the fire of the Lord' (i.e. lightning) 'fell', and the sacrifice was burnt up. The crowd of assembled Israelites immediately declared themselves on Elijah's side. He had taunted them with trying to serve both gods at once. Now they cried: 'Yahweh is God', and they took the priests of Melkart to the foot of the mountain and slaughtered them.

We must regard this strange incident in the light of the ideas of the people of that time. They believed in the real existence of both Yahweh and Melkart and the result of the contest proved to the Israelites that their God was the more powerful; he had sent the fire and showed that he accepted Elijah's sacrifice, whereas Melkart was powerless to help his own people. Shortly afterwards there was heavy rain; the drought was at an end. Elijah may have had this in mind in preparing his sacrifice, for it was a common idea among people who believed in magic that pouring out water would bring rain. Some people think that it was not water which Elijah poured over his sacrifice; it is unlikely that there would be a spring at the top of Mount Carmel after three years of drought. There is some evidence that the priests used crude oil to set light to their offerings, which would catch fire in the heat of the sun or if struck by lightning. Perhaps Elijah knew of a local supply and drenched his altar with this.

Elijah sent a warning to Ahab to get back to Samaria before he was caught in the river valley when the floods came, and the king told Jezebel what had happened. She was furious at the slaughter of her priests and vowed to kill Elijah. He fled south in fear, through the territory of Israel and Judah, until he came to the Sinai desert. It was as if he wanted to get away to the place where the covenant had been made between the nation and God in the time of Moses. He was very depressed and wanted to die, for he thought that he was the only one left who was faithful. As he took shelter in a cave, he watched the violent forces of nature. There was an earthquake, then a storm of wind swept through the rocks, then came lightning. But he could not find God in these. Then he heard something like a gentle whisper—'a low murmuring sound' is one translation. Perhaps after the noise of the storm there was absolute stillness. It was in this silence that he received a message. He was told not to sulk there but to return and get on with his job. He was to appoint a new king over Syria, a king over Israel to take the place of Ahab and a successor, Elisha, to carry on his own work. Elijah had learnt a lesson which was uncommon in those times—that the voice of God was not to be found in violent ways like the powerful forces of nature but in the stillness, speaking within a man's own heart and mind.

Elijah challenged Ahab on another occasion also, when the king wanted a vineyard which belonged to a neighbour of his named Naboth. Ahab asked for it and even promised to pay for it or to give Naboth another in exchange, but he refused to part with it. Ahab flung himself down on his bed and sulked. Jezebel scornfully asked him: 'Are you really the ruler of Israel? *I* will get you Naboth's vineyard'. She was used to the tyrannical rule of her father in Phoenicia and expected Ahab to act in the same way. So she sent instructions in the king's name that Naboth was to be accused of disloyalty towards Yahweh and treason against the king. Her plan succeeded and Naboth was stoned to death. His body was flung outside the city, to be eaten by the wild pariah dogs. Ahab went along to survey his new possession. But in the pathway stood Elijah, who denounced him as Nathan had denounced David. Elijah promised that both Ahab and Jezebel would suffer a similar fate to that of Naboth.

So Elijah stood almost alone for two principles—faithfulness to Yahweh against the introduction of a foreign god, and the rights of the common people against the oppression of a tyrant. These two were closely related, for, unlike the nations who worshipped other gods, the Hebrews realised that Yahweh wanted right conduct and morals from his people.

Elijah's successor, Elisha, is not such a great figure. He was more influential at court than Elijah had been and was consulted by various kings of Israel who succeeded Ahab. He was visited by Naaman, a captain in the army of Syria who had a skin disease of some kind. Elisha told him to get cured by bathing in the river Jordan. Several miraculous acts are told of Elisha, some of which sound rather exaggerated, and they are not of great importance for Hebrew religion.

Soon after Elijah had denounced Ahab, the king was killed while fighting against Syria. A man named Jehu, who had been a general in Ahab's army, later seized the throne and started a new dynasty. He massacred all he could find of Ahab's family. A gruesome story is told of the end of Jezebel. She was watching Jehu's entry into Samaria from an upstairs window and taunted him with being a murderer. Jehu ordered her attendants to throw her down into the road and he drove his chariot over her body and went in to celebrate his triumph with a banquet. Then he remembered Jezebel—'after all, she is a king's daughter', he said—but when his men went to bury her they found that the dogs had eaten her flesh. Jehu's reign was a disastrous one for Israel. The country was in a state of disorder for a long time afterwards, with several revolutions and with usurpers seizing the throne. In the 120 years after Ahab there were twelve kings in Samaria, the last five succeeding one another in the course of seven years. Then the country, in this weak and disordered state, was threatened by Assyria.

This eastern power, with its capital Nineveh on the Tigris, was on the warpath. The petty kingdoms into which the area around Palestine had been divided stood between Assyria and its great rival, Egypt. It was essential that the power which was to be master of the Middle East should conquer these. Israel and Syria made an alliance to defy the Assyrian king, Tiglath-Pileser III. So he led his army against Syria; the king was killed in battle and Damascus the capital taken, in 732 B.C. The king of Israel hastily submitted and promised to pay tribute. But as soon as the Assyrian king's back was turned, he began to plot with Egypt. A new Assyrian monarch, Shalmaneser V, brought his forces westwards and in 722 B.C. Samaria was captured after a long siege. An Assyrian governor was set over the district and the kingdom of Israel ceased to exist. The principal people were deported to Assyria and settled in various places in Mesopotamia. This was the usual practice in those times when a country was defeated, to ensure that the people would not revolt. Those Israelites who were taken off were not firm enough to keep their national identity or their religion and nothing more is heard about them. They probably mingled with their conquerors. The Israelites who were left in the country around Samaria had to put up with colonists and settlers who were brought in from Assyria, These foreigners brought their own religion—the worship of Mesopotamian gods—with them. When lions came up from the country-side and attacked them, they thought it was because they did not know 'the god of the land', so an Israelite priest came from Assyria to instruct them. The race and the religion of the people in the territory which had been the kingdom of Israel thus became very mixed. The people of the southern kingdom despised them for this. Judah continued as an independent nation for about another 130 years.

While these events were happening in Israel—conflict with other nations, revolutions and eventually conquest by the Assyrians—conditions inside the country were very bad. We have evidence of this from prophets of a new type who appeared in Israel. We have accounts in the Old Testament historical books of the activities and message of earlier prophets—Nathan, Elijah, Elisha—but they themselves left nothing in writing. But about 750 B.C. there were prophets whose words have been preserved in books, set down either by themselves or by their followers. The first of these 'writing prophets' was Amos. He lived originally in the southern kingdom of Judah. He was a shepherd on a farm and had the job also of looking after the sycamore trees which were cultivated, producing a fruit like a fig. When he left the simple life of the country and travelled to Bethel, where Jeroboam had set up the bull image, he was horrified at what he saw in the life of the city. Outwardly the nation appeared to be rich and prosperous; trade was good and the economy of the country seemed to be sound. But the wealth which this prosperity brought was enjoyed by comparatively few of the people. There was a great gulf between the luxury of the rich and the poverty of the common people. Amos saw that the rulers and rich people oppressed the poor who had to work for them. If a man fell into debt and was unable to pay, he could be sold into slavery by his creditor and the same treatment was sometimes meted out to his family as well. A small farmer who was faced with a loss because of a bad harvest was often compelled to sell his land to a rich and powerful neighbour and so great estates developed which were managed by a few wealthy owners. Even the law courts were corrupt. Justice was a mockery and a man who could not afford to bribe the judge lost his case.

Amos stood up and condemned the injustice and the exploitation of the poor. He spoke scornfully of the luxury of the rich classes. He described them as idling in Samaria, 'lying on their beds of ivory and sprawling on their couches'; they had the best meat from the farms for their banquets, while listening to music and using the most expensive perfumes. But, he added, they had never a thought for the misery of the people.

What particularly appalled Amos was that the rulers and rich nobles were outwardly very religious people. They gave their sacrifices, paid their tithes to the priests, attended all the regular ceremonies, made their prayers and prided themselves that they were pleasing to God. But Amos said, speaking as though they were the words of Yahweh himself: 'I don't want your feasts and solemn ceremonies. When you make your sacrifices and present your gifts, I will not accept them. I will not listen to your prayers and your hymns'. Instead, Amos declared: 'Let justice roll on like a river and righteousness like a stream in full flood'.

He added a note of stern warning. The Hebrews were talking at this time about the 'day of the Lord'. They looked forward to a time when judgment would come upon the nations. They thought that this would be a day of glory for themselves, since they had kept faithful to God, but a day of disaster for other peoples. Amos condemned this idea. He held that Yahweh was interested not only in Israel but the other nations around. He denounced the evils in these one by one—Syria, Philistia, Phoenicia, Edom, Ammon, Moab. Then he came to Judah, and finally to Israel, declaring that their punishment would be all the more severe because they had had the opportunity of knowing God and following the Law, but had misused it. For them the day of the Lord would be 'not a day of light but a day of darkness'. The people of Israel, especially the rulers, could not escape.

Amos' words naturally brought him into conflict with the political and religious leaders of the nation. The priests who were in charge of Bethel were enraged. The priest Amaziah reported his words to the king (Jeroboam II), saying that Amos was guilty of treason. The priest ordered Amos to get back to Judah and utter his prophecies there. Amos replied: 'I am not one of the sons of the prophets'. He refused to be associated with the excited companies who still roamed the countryside, he said he was a countryman working on a farm: 'Yahweh took me from following flock and said: "Go and preach to my people Israel".' He warned the priest that he, with the rulers of the nation, would be taken off to a foreign country. He could see that the security of Israel would not last long. The power of Assyria was increasing and that great empire would soon swallow up the small kingdoms of Palestine. Thirty years later, in 722 B.C., this did happen as he had foreseen and the strength of Samaria was shattered, never to recover.

Amos thus stands out, like Elijah, as one who dared to face the anger of priests and rulers and showed the hollowness of religion if it was not accompanied by justice and a high standard of morality. A few years later there was another prophet in Israel, Hosea. He denounced the way in which the Israelite kings tried to gain in turn the help of Egypt or Assyria, seeking to play off one great power against the other. Such tactics would not help them, for like Amos he could see destruction coming upon the nation. He declared that the country was corrupt, with robbery and other crimes widespread and bandits roaming the land. The kings and self-indulgent princes were largely to blame, setting a bad example to the people. He said that Yahweh scorned the images which they had set up and had no pleasure in their worship. But Hosea had a more tender note in his teaching as well. He pictured God as a father, who taught his young child to walk. 'When Israel was a child I loved him and called my son out of Egypt'. But in spite of the tender care and love which Yahweh had given them, the people had deserted him. Yet God was still anxious to heal them and restore the nation.

We can see from the words of Amos and Hosea that it

is incorrect to think of the prophets as men whose chief concern was with foretelling the future. Their message was directed towards their own times. They said that God wanted justice and mercy, honest conduct of business and righteousness in national affairs, rather than mere religious ceremonies, sacrifices and prayers that meant nothing. This idea of God as interested in right conduct was not to be found anywhere else in the ancient world. Only among the Hebrews did true religion become associated with morality. This is well summarised in the words of a later prophet, in the book of Micah. He first asks a question: 'How shall I approach God?—with burnt offerings, sacrifices of animals, even the giving of my own son in human sacrifice?' His answer was a different one from this popular one. What God wants from men, he says, is for them 'to act justly, to love mercy and kindness and to walk humbly with God'.

PASSAGES REFERRED TO IN THIS CHAPTER:

Elijah and the priests of Melkart at Mount Carmel: 1 *Kings* 18.17 to 18.40.
Elijah at Horeb (Sinai) finds a message from God: 1 *Kings* 19.8 to 19.18.
Ahab and the vineyard of Naboth: 1 *Kings* 21.1 to 21.20.
The fall of Samaria to the Assyrians: 2 *Kings* 17.1 to 17.6.
The new inhabitants of Samaria: 2 *Kings* 17.24 to 17.29.
Amos' denunciation of the selfish rich: *Amos* 6.1 to 6.7.
Amos denounces sacrifices and calls for justice: *Amos* 5.21 to 5.24.
Amos' conflict with the priest at Bethel: *Amos* 7.10 to 7.17.
Hosea's picture of Yahweh's care for Israel: *Hosea* 11.1 to 11.4.
A prophet's summary of true religion: *Micah* 6.6 to 6.8.

7

The Kingdom of Judah

While these events were taking place in Israel, ending with the destruction of the country at the hands of the Assyrians, the southern kingdom of Judah had a somewhat less disturbed history. It had two advantages which its northern neighbour lacked—a capital city, with the temple which Solomon had built, and a royal line. The kings in Judah were the descendants of David, although they often had little of his greatness, and the people of the south considered that their monarchy was the only true succession.

The fortunes of Judah were varied. Sometimes the kingdom was at peace with Israel, sometimes at enmity. A crisis occurred in 735 B.C., when Israel and Syria made an alliance, hoping to present a common front against the advance westwards of Assyria. They considered that the help of Judah was essential and marched against Jerusalem to force that kingdom to join them. The king of Judah, Ahaz, was alarmed and thought of calling in the help of Assyria against this threat. This would have been a very foolish action, to invite this powerful empire to interfere in the affairs of Palestine. Ahaz was advised against this step by a very remarkable man who was a prophet and also a statesman, Isaiah. He told Ahaz not

to be afraid of the two kings who were threatening him—
'burnt-out firebrands', he scornfully called them—but to
trust in Yahweh. He offered a sign of his confidence. He
said that a woman who was shortly to have a child would
give him the name of Immanuel, which meant 'God is
with us'. A name meant much in the east and this would
show that the mother was sure that God had not deserted
the nation. Before the boy was old enough to know how
'to reject evil and choose good'—we should say 'to come
to years of discretion'—the danger would have passed
and the lands of Israel and Syria would be swept away.
Isaiah could see that the outcome of their plotting together
would be conquest by Assyria. As we have seen, three
years after this Damascus fell and ten years later Samaria
suffered the same fate. The northern kingdom of the
Hebrews came to an end and Judah was left standing
alone. All that remained of the kingdom and empire of
Solomon was this small state, about 90 miles in length and
50 miles across. (From this time onwards the inhabitants
may be referred to as Jews, for this name means simply
'men of Judah'.)

Isaiah also gave advice to another king, Hezekiah, the
successor of Ahaz. In 701 B.C. the Assyrian king
Sennacherib invaded Palestine, to put down movements
of revolt among the small nations which had submitted
to him. Judah defied him, so he besieged Jerusalem and
sent an officer to demand the surrender of the city. This
man first made a speech to the people manning the walls.
He derided the trust which they placed in their God. The
gods of the other nations, he told them, had proved help-
less to save their people and Jerusalem also would have to
submit to the Assyrians. The people refused to answer him,
so he next sent a letter to the king emphasising the same
arguments. Hezekiah consulted Isaiah, who told him to
ignore Sennacherib's threats. He was confident that the
danger would pass and that Jerusalem would not be

taken. That night, says the Old Testament writer, 'the angel of the Lord' went through the Assyrian camp and in the morning it was full of dead men. A Greek historian, writing about this later, said that the Assyrians were attacked by field-mice, which ate through the bow-strings of the archers. Probably the mice brought plague, which swept through the Assyrian army. Whatever the cause, their force was disabled and Sennacherib went home; for the time at least the threat to Judah from the east was removed.

Isaiah was different in some ways from the prophets we have seen so far. Unlike Elijah, who was a kind of hermit living in the desert, and Amos, who was a farm labourer, Isaiah was a nobleman, accustomed to attendance at the court of the king. His book contains his own account of his call to be a prophet. One day he was in the courtyard of the temple when sacrifice was being offered. Smoke was rising from the altars and the temple choirs were chanting their praises to God. He fell into a trance in which he had a vision of Yahweh on his throne. Around him were his attendants, who hailed him as holy. So great was the impression on Isaiah that the whole place seemed to be shaken. His first reaction was to declare that he was unworthy to see God. 'I am impure and live among an impure people', he declared. A seraph (a winged figure who acted as Yahweh's messenger) flew down, purified him and took away his unworthiness. Then he heard Yahweh asking: 'Whom shall I send? Who will go as my messenger?' and without hesitation he answered: 'Here am I. Send me'. Then he was told how his work would be received—that the people would be obstinate and would not respond; they would become even more dull and unwilling to listen. 'For how long?' he asked and the answer was until the land was devastated and the people removed into exile.

This is a dramatic description of Isaiah's own experience. He realised that God was calling him but his work would seem a failure; he was to go on persisting in spite of this. He continued as a prophet for forty years from that time. In times of crisis such as those which faced Ahaz and Hezekiah he advised the king and tried to guide the nation. He told the people that they should not rely on the might of Assyria. He held that it was foolish for the little kingdom of Judah to attempt to play at world politics. That way would be disastrous. The true mission of the Jews was to keep faithful to God, even if that meant an unimportant place in the world of that day. One sentence in his book sums up his message: 'In quietness and in confidence shall be your strength'.

Isaiah had much to say also about conditions inside the country. Like Amos in the north, he denounced the injustice of rulers, the oppression of the poor by the rich and the way in which people thought that they were pleasing God because of their sacrifices and religious ceremonies. To him Yahweh was holy and could not endure evil actions among his worshippers. Isaiah declared that the people were like the old cities of wickedness, Sodom and Gomorrah, in the time of the patriarchs. He said that Yahweh had had enough of all their sacrifices, their burning of incense, their solemn assemblies and their religious festivals. He did not want them trampling the courts of the temple and when they prayed he would not listen—because the hands that they stretched out were stained with bloodshed. What God wanted was for them to turn from their evil ways and do good, to practise justice and goodness, especially to help widows and orphans, the most neglected sections of eastern society.

We do not know whether Isaiah's words were heeded or what finally happened to him. Jewish tradition stated that he was put to death in the reign of Manasseh, a bad king who followed Hezekiah. Manasseh was succeeded by Josiah, a very different kind of king. He carried out a religious reformation throughout Judah. There were many places in the country where altars had been set up and priests made sacrifices to Yahweh, often on hills where the Canaanites had formerly worshipped their gods. Josiah decreed that sacrifices should be made only at the temple at Jerusalem. The altars throughout the country were torn down and the bull image which Jeroboam had set up at Bethel was destroyed. The priests who officiated at these places were brought to Jerusalem and given less important positions. Josiah based his reforms on a book now in the Old Testament called Deuteronomy, much of which had been written a few years before, in the reign of Manasseh, and hidden in a room in the temple. This book not only laid down laws about worship and sacrifice but also emphasised the teaching of the prophets—that God wanted a devotion that showed itself in the practice of justice and faithfulness and common kindness among men. It also contains a passage which became the central theme of the Jewish religion: 'The Lord our God is one; and you must love God with all your heart and soul and strength'.

Judah continued to be subject to Assyria and had to pay an annual tribute to keep the foreign armies off her soil. But Assyria was declining as a new power gained strength, that of Babylon on the Euphrates. This city had been part of the Assyrian empire but the people revolted and declared their country independent. Joined by Medes from further east, the Babylonian forces captured Nineveh, the capital of Assyria, in 612 B.C. The rulers of Egypt took advantage of the unsettled state of affairs and invaded Palestine. The Jewish kingdom became a province of the Egyptian empire for a short time. Conditions inside Judah were very bad. The teaching of Isaiah and the reforms of Josiah were largely ignored and people resorted to their old bad ways.

It has been said that when Nineveh fell a yell of triumph went up all over the Middle East. There is a small book in the Old Testament (Nahum) which consists of poems exulting over the destruction of Nineveh. But the little nations shouted too soon, for they found that they had only exchanged one tyranny for another. The Babylonians soon advanced westwards and took over most of the lands which had been under the Assyrians. The Egyptians were driven out of Palestine and Judah became subject to Babylon. Within three years the Jewish king rebelled. The nations around which were friendly to Babylon attacked Jerusalem and the Babylonian king Nebuchadrezzar himself marched west. In 597 B.C. he besieged Jerusalem for three months and took the city. Many of the leading men were deported to Babylon and a puppet king was put on the throne of Judah. But within nine years, encouraged by Egypt, he was plotting to free his nation. To put down the revolt Nebuchadrezzar again came to Palestine. After a siege of eighteen months Jerusalem fell and this time the Babylonian king decided to put an end to this troublesome little nation. The city was plundered, the principal buildings set on fire and the walls broken down. The temple which Solomon had built nearly 400 years before was destroyed. The leading nobles and priests were put to death. The king was captured and blinded and taken as a prisoner to Babylon. Large numbers of the inhabitants were taken away as captives, although people were left in the country districts around Jerusalem to cultivate the land, but as a nation Judah ceased to exist (586 B.C.).

During these events one man stands out among the weak kings and the plots of the rulers—the prophet Jeremiah. Like Isaiah 150 years before, he denounced the evils of his day. He used to go into the temple court at Jerusalem when the people were gathering for a festival and tell them to change their ways. He accused them of oppression of the innocent, of bloodshed, lying, unfaithfulness to Yahweh and the worship of other gods. Yet they considered that Yahweh would protect them, as they had the temple. They came with their sacrifices, to deliver them from danger, but continued to do all these evil things. The temple, he declared, had become a den of robbers, like a cave among the mountains where brigands met to share out their loot.

Such talk did not make him popular and the authorities tried to silence him. On one occasion he was put under house-arrest, so he dictated his words to Baruch, a scribe, and told him to read them to the crowds in the temple court. The nobles reported the matter to the king, who ordered one of them to read to him what Jeremiah had said. But the reader had not proceeded very far when the king seized the scroll, slashed at it with his knife and flung it into the fire. When this was reported to Jeremiah, he dictated to Baruch all over again, adding some fresh denunciations of the king.

Jeremiah not only spoke about the religion of the people and their social conduct. He was concerned also about the political situation. He warned the king and the nation about the consequences of their defiance of Babylon and their reliance on Egypt. He could see that the result of such a policy would be destruction. He told the king personally that he was simply deceiving himself and that if he persisted Jerusalem would be captured by the Babylonians. It was better to 'serve the king of Babylon and live'. He counselled the people to submit and to surrender to the invading armies even when Jerusalem was under siege. Only in that way, he said, could Judah keep its identity and preserve what was most precious in the nation. Otherwise, if they continued to resist, they would lose everything—the city and the temple, nation-hood and religion alike. He declared that it was the will of Yahweh that the countries of Palestine should submit to Nebuchadrezzar, for he was an instrument in the hand of God.

For such words Jeremiah was regarded as a traitor; his fellow-countrymen believed that he was in league with the Babylonians. He was imprisoned and attempts were made on his life. They did not dare to put a prophet to death deliberately, but on one occasion he was flung down a dried-up but very muddy well. He was rescued by an Ethiopian servant in the palace, who knotted together rags and sheets and pulled him up. Some of the Jews escaped to Egypt just before the final overthrow of Jerusalem in 586 B.C. and, against his will, took Jeremiah with them, for they thought that he would go over to the Babylonians when they entered the city. The last report we have of him is that he was protesting in Egypt against the way in which the Jews there took part in the worship of Egyptian gods. They thought that they could combine the religion of Yahweh with reverence for the gods of the country in which they were living. Jewish tradition said that Jeremiah was eventually stoned to death in Egypt.

Jeremiah was an unwilling prophet, for by nature he was a shy and modest man and shrank from public life. He preferred to live quietly in the country rather than become involved in political activity in the city. When he felt called by God to be a prophet, he declared that he was too young and was unworthy. Yet he knew that he had to speak; if he stopped, he said, it was as if there was a fire within him which impelled him to go on. At times he doubted his own call and wondered if God himself had deceived him. He had the pain of seeing the country which he loved going blindly on its path to ruin and his warnings scorned. Jeremiah is often considered a pessimist but he was really a man who saw the truth and dared to speak it at a time when it was unpopular.

He told the Jews that they were responsible for their own condition. They tended to shift the blame on to their ancestors. They had a popular proverb: 'The parents have eaten sour grapes and the children's teeth are set on edge'. That kind of talk had got to stop, said Jeremiah. The man who does evil is himself responsible, not his ancestors, and he will have to suffer the result of his wrongdoing.

There was also hope in his message. He sent a letter to the first batch of exiles, who had been taken to Babylon in 597 B.C., urging them to settle down among their conquerors, for they would be able eventually to return to Palestine. He thought that Yahweh had great plans for the future of the nation. He looked for a time when Israel and Judah would be united again and he likened God to a shepherd who collects his flock and leads them safely home. The most remarkable passage in his writings is a short paragraph in which he spoke of a new covenant. From the earliest times there had been such a compact between Yahweh and the Hebrews. The conditions which they had to observe had been laid down in writing, first on stone tablets in the time of Moses and then in later books. Jeremiah saw that the Jews had not kept their part of the covenant. Yet, he said, God would not give them up. He would make a new covenant, in which the laws would be written on men's hearts and minds. There would no longer be a need for outward commands and instruction about God, for men would know him for themselves. There would be fellowship between God and men and their sins would be quite forgiven. Jeremiah never saw the fulfilment of his hopes but his vision remained as a great ideal for the nation and for the individual.

PASSAGES REFERRED TO IN THIS CHAPTER:

Isaiah's account of his call: *Isaiah* 6.1 to 6.12.
Isaiah's denunciation of the religion of his day and his call for justice: *Isaiah* 1.10 to 1.17.

Isaiah advises king Ahaz: *Isaiah* 7.1 to 7.6 and 7.10 to 7.17.

Sennacherib demands the surrender of Jerusalem: 2 *Kings* 18.28 to 18.31 and 19.1 to 19.7.

The destruction of Sennacherib's army: 2 *Kings* 19.35 to 19.37.

The reforms of Josiah: 2 *Kings* 23.15 to 23.25.

The first capture of Jerusalem (597 B.C.): 2 *Kings* 24.10 to 24.17.

The capture of Jerusalem by Nebuchadrezzar and the destruction of the temple: 2 *Kings* 25.1 to 25.12.

Jeremiah denounces the misuse of the temple: *Jeremiah* 7.1 to 7.11.

Jeremiah's advice to the exiles in Babylon: *Jeremiah* 29.1 to 29.14.

Jeremiah's prophecies are destroyed by the Jewish king: *Jeremiah* 36.

Jeremiah's hope of a new covenant: *Jeremiah* 31.31 to 31.34.

8

The Jews in Exile

In Babylon the deported Jews found conditions very different from those in their own land. Babylon was a very large city, with wide streets with palaces, mansions, shops and temples to the gods and with strong fortifications. Some of the Jews were sold as slaves in the city, while others lived on the plains which were watered by the rivers and canals. Many of them kept together in communities and they seem to have been fairly peaceful and prosperous. They were allowed to practise their own customs. Some of them adopted the ways and even the religion of the Babylonians, but others remained faithful to Yahweh and regarded their exile as a punishment for the sins of Judah. They did not attempt to stir up trouble in the land of their conquerors. Perhaps they remembered the advice which Jeremiah had given them.

The Jews in exile were more steadfast than the people of the northern kingdom had been, when they were deported to Assyria in 722 B.C. Most of them wished to maintain their national identity and their religion even in a foreign land. There was one great difficulty in this: the temple at Jerusalem had been destroyed. This was the centre of their religion and since the time of Josiah it had been the only official place for sacrifice. The Jews had believed that God could be found especially in this holy place. They now had to face the question: Could they still worship without the elaborate temple ceremonies and without approaching God with sacrifices? Would he be with them in a foreign country? The Jews began to meet together for prayer to God. They read together from the scrolls which the scribes and priests had brought with them—the records of their history and the words of the prophets. They held these meetings particularly on the Sabbath. They had of course no separate buildings of their own in which to meet, so they gathered in the open-air or in private houses. This was the beginning of what later became known as the synagogue (a Greek word meaning assembly). They were also distinguished from the Babylonians by their practice of fasting at set times, their refusal to eat certain kinds of foods, their observing set hours of prayer each day and keeping the Sabbath as a day free from work, as far as that was possible. In these ways they tried to maintain their loyalty to Yahweh and his laws.

There was much literary activity among some of the exiled Jews who were professional writers or scribes. Two documents relating the early history of the Hebrews had already been combined before the exile and these were now edited and made into one connected account. The priests put together the various laws and the regulations about religious observances and inserted these at various points in the narratives. Thus the historical books, telling the story of their race from the time of Abraham to the kings, gradually took the form which they now have in the Old Testament. These books were not written by any one man but are the result of a long process by which various traditions and documents were collected and edited.

Some of the exiles wrote poems, which were later included in the book of Psalms. One of these (*Psalm* 137) expresses the sorrow of the Jews as they sat 'by the rivers of Babylon' and remembered Jerusalem. The Babylonians taunted them to 'sing one of the songs of Zion', but they declared that they could not 'sing the Lord's song in a foreign land'. The poet expresses his love for Jerusalem and his longing to see the city again. Unfortunately he finishes on a vindictive note, calling down vengeance on those who took part in the destruction of Jerusalem.

Although some of the Jews settled down fairly comfortably in Babylonia, many of them hoped for a return to Palestine. This expectation was sustained by two prophets. One of them was a priest named Ezekiel. He had been taken to Babylon at the first capture of Jerusalem in 597 B.C. and had settled about fifty miles south of the city with a colony of Jews to whom he acted as leader and adviser. He tried to get his fellow-countrymen to recognise their own responsibility for the calamity which had befallen them, emphasising that a man was responsible for his own misdeeds. He repeated the words of Jeremiah, that they were not to blame their ancestors for their present state. If a man is righteous, he said, he is accepted by God, no matter what kind of man his father had been. If one does wrong, he is condemned for his own action, whether his father was a good or a bad man. He added that if a bad man turns away from his evil life he is accepted by God. Ezekiel also hoped that when the Jews got back to Judah it would be possible to start the sacrificial system again and he drew plans for a new temple and a restored city. Like Jeremiah, he also expected that the kingdoms of Israel and Judah would be reunited, but this hope was never fulfilled.

Ezekiel had some remarkable experiences and seems to have gone at times into a state of trance in which he saw strange visions. In one passage in his book he says that he visited a valley which was full of dry bones; perhaps it was the site of an ancient battle. Yahweh spoke to him and asked him if these bones could live. Only God knew that, he answered. He was then told to preach to the bones and as he looked they came together until the valley was filled with skeletons. Then flesh came upon them; but they were still lifeless bodies. Then he was told to call upon the wind, and as it swept through the valley breath and life came into the bodies and they were a great force of living men once more. That, said Ezekiel, is what you Jews are like. You say in despair that there is no life left in the nation. But Yahweh will put his spirit in you and you will live again and will be able to go back to your country. Ezekiel used a play upon words to enforce his message, for the same Hebrew word stood for the wind which blew in the valley, the breath which came into the bodies and made them living, and the Spirit of God which would come upon the nation. This was Ezekiel's hope for them.

The other prophet is a man whose name we do not know. His writings are to be found in sixteen chapters of the book of Isaiah. This long book, sixty-six chapters in all, contains the teaching of at least three different prophets. Only the first thirty-nine chapters relate to the time of Isaiah of Jerusalem, in the reigns of Ahaz and Hezekiah, 150 years before the exile. Chapters 40 to 55 plainly refer to conditions in Babylon and have nothing to do with Isaiah himself. The writer was a prophet who spoke to the Jews in exile; he is generally referred to as Second-Isaiah (or Deutero-Isaiah—the Greek word for second) but we have no idea what his real name was. (Chapters 56–66 are from even later writers.) There are other books also in the Old Testament which contain the writings of more than one prophet. This came about because a very early scribe who was copying a book had not completely filled his parchment roll when that book was finished, so he continued on the same roll by copying another book by a different man.

The opening verses of chapter 40 are words of consolation to the Jews in exile. 'Comfort, my people', God says. The prophet is to 'speak tenderly to Jerusalem', for the time of strife is over and the Jews have suffered quite enough. The prophet then pictures a messenger proclaiming the return of the exiles and preparing a way, just as a herald used to be sent forward when a king was to visit his dominions. All difficulties would be overcome—'every valley raised up and every mountain and hill levelled out', as he poetically puts it. He tells the herald to ascend a high mountain so that Jerusalem may hear the good news. But he pictures God as coming not as a stern judge denouncing the people for their faithlessness, as the pre-exilic prophets had done, but as a shepherd, dealing kindly with his flock.

Included in this book of Second-Isaiah there are four poems about someone who is called the servant of Yahweh. These are often referred to as the Servant-Songs. The writer pictures a man who was called by God to serve him and his fellow-men faithfully, even if this meant suffering and eventually his own death. In one of the poems the servant is said to be uncomplaining and gentle towards the weak, but he must not be discouraged until he has established justice in the world. His life of service would bring men to God. But the servant was not only to restore the Jewish nation; he was also to be 'a light to the Gentiles' (the name used for non-Jews), so that the knowledge of God would reach the whole world—'that my salvation may reach to the ends of the earth'.

The writer emphasises that this mission of the servant would involve suffering. In the last of the four poems (chapter 53) he first pictures the servant as exalted by God, to the astonishment of men. Yet, he goes on, the servant was not attractive to look at; he was 'despised and rejected', 'a man of sorrow, humbled by suffering'. Men turned aside from him, as if there was something repulsive in his appearance. The servant went to his fate without resistance or complaint. He was as innocent as a lamb in the slaughter-house. Eventually the servant died. Yet in the end he was victorious, for men realised that his sufferings were for their sake.

It is uncertain whom the writer was thinking of in these poems. He may have had an individual in mind and it has been suggested that he was thinking of Jeremiah, who had suffered so much at the hands of his fellow-countrymen. It is more likely that he did not mean any particular individual but was portraying the Jews in general. In one place he writes that God said: 'You are my servant Israel, in whom I shall win glory'. The prophet hoped that there would be at least some members of the Jewish nation who would be disciplined and purified by all their sufferings in exile and that they would learn that their mission was to help the world to a knowledge of God and even the Gentiles would benefit from their loyalty and endurance. The last poem in particular seems to reflect the sufferings that the Israelites had had to undergo throughout their history. The nation had indeed been 'despised and rejected' by other peoples. In the Babylonian exile Judah appeared to be annihilated, just as in the poem the servant was put to death. The writer hoped that the Jews would be able to bear their sufferings in a noble spirit and that as a result the nations of the world would realise this and would be brought to the knowledge of God.

The experiences of the Jews in exile led to a great step forward in their idea of God. This arose from their contact with the Babylonian religion. They witnessed the ceremonies in honour of the Babylonian gods and watched the processions through the streets. Deutero-Isaiah ridiculed the gods who had to be carried about by their worshippers. The Jews' idea of Yahweh the invisible was greatly superior to these. But the old belief still persisted that God was limited to the territory of his people. But they had found that they could still be loyal to Yahweh and could meet him when they gathered for prayer and reading together, even though they were removed from their own land and their temple had been destroyed. They had not left him back in Palestine, so he must be everywhere and men could worship and serve him in any land. The next step was: therefore he is the only God. The gods of the Babylonians and other nations simply did not exist and there was only one God, whom they worshipped. This is monotheism and it is in the writings of Deutero-Isaiah that there is the first clear statement of this belief. There is the declaration: 'I am Yahweh and there is no other. Besides me there is no god.' This is the climax in the development of thought among the Hebrews—first a tribal god, in the nomadic period and the time of the exodus from Egypt; then a national god, in the time of the kings; and then a universal God and finally only one God. The Jews thoroughly learnt the lesson and never afterwards did they think there were any other gods but Yahweh, although for hundreds of years they were the only people in the world who thought in this way.

One conclusion from the belief in one God was that the world owed its existence to him. Deutero-Isaiah declared that it was Yahweh who 'created the skies and fashioned the earth and gave breath to the people upon it'. It was during the exile that the Jews came across the Babylonian myth about the creation, which told how the world was made by the gods, but as the result of their rivalry and quarrels. The Jews took the pagan, unworthy elements out of the account, rewrote the story of creation as the work of one God and eventually put it at the beginning of the first book of their Bible.

But deliverance for the Jews in exile was not far off. A new power was arising. To the east of Babylon was the country of Persia. A king there named Cyrus had extended his rule over the empire of the Medes, to the north of Babylonia. His territory then stretched eastwards as far as the borders of India, northwards to the Caspian Sea and westwards to include parts of Asia Minor. In 546 B.C. he turned his attention to Babylon and the capital city fell to him without a struggle in 539. The Babylonian empire gave way to the Persian, the largest that the Middle East had seen up to that time.

It was probably the advance of Cyrus that made the Jews in exile hope for a release. Deutero-Isaiah refers to Cyrus by name in two places, saying that he had been chosen by Yahweh to carry out his purpose for the benefit of the Jews. The prophet considered that God was concerned not only with Israel but with the activities of other nations and rulers as well. Soon after capturing Babylon Cyrus issued a decree which was set down on a clay cylinder which has been found. It declared that Marduk (the chief Babylonian deity) permitted the return to their lands of all peoples and their gods. This meant that the Jews, among others, might end their captivity and return to Palestine if they wished. This was sound policy on the part of Cyrus, for he did not want groups of discontented and possibly rebellious foreigners under his rule. So the Jews now had the opportunity, after nearly fifty years of exile, to start afresh and rebuild their nation.

PASSAGES REFERRED TO IN THIS CHAPTER:

Ezekiel's vision of the dry bones: *Ezekiel* 37.1 to 37.14.
A psalm written during the exile: *Psalm* 137.
The hope of a return from exile: *Isaiah* 40.1 to 40.11.
The servant of Yahweh: *Isaiah* 42.1 to 42.4.

The suffering and triumph of the servant: *Isaiah* 52.13 to
  52.15 and 53.
Yayweh's use of Cyrus: *Isaiah* 45.1 to 45.4.
The statement of monotheism: *Isaiah* 45.5 to 45.7.
God as creator of the world: *Isaiah* 42.5 to 42.9.
The proclamation of Cyrus: *Ezra* 1.

9

The Return from Exile

Not all the Jews in Babylonia took the opportunity given them by the decree of Cyrus. Probably the majority of the original exiles had died by this time and the younger Jews, born in Babylon, had less interest in Palestine. Some of them had settled down to business life and had no wish to leave the comforts of civilisation for a precarious venture in what to most of them would be a strange country. So it was a small and somewhat dispirited company which made the long journey to Palestine, and what they found on arriving at Jerusalem further disheartened them. The Jews who had remained in Judah were very despondent. It was a time of famine and scarcity and they were almost surrounded by hostile peoples. The city was still largely in ruins and no effort had been made to rebuild the temple. The first band of returned exiles probably set up the altar of burnt offering, so that the priests could make the usual sacrifices, but no building was erected for some time.

About seventeen years after the return two prophets, Haggai and Zechariah, reproached the people because they had homes to live in but there was no house for God. They held that the temple was the centre of their national religious life and that without it Yahweh could not be fully worshipped. So the people of Jerusalem set about building a temple, although they realised that it could never equal the glory of the one built by Solomon. An offer to help came from the Samaritans—descendants of the tribes of the northern kingdom who had been left when the Assyrians had deported the leading people in 722 B.C. They said that they worshipped the same God as the Jews and claimed that they were true Israelites. But the Jewish leaders refused to accept their help, so the Samaritans did all they could to hinder the work. When the Persian governor of Palestine heard about events in Jerusalem, he enquired what the Jews were doing, asked who gave them permission and then sent to Babylon to see if this was in order. Cyrus had been succeeded by Darius and he found the decree of Cyrus and wrote back that the Jews should be given every encouragement. The temple was finally completed and dedicated in 516–515 B.C.

The situation in Judah for the next seventy years is obscure. The community of Jews remained in a weak and disheartened state. When they tried to rebuild the walls of the city, about 450 B.C., the Samaritans and other opponents sent a letter of complaint to the Persian king, Artaxerxes, declaring that as soon as the Jews had fortified the city they would not pay their taxes and would rebel. The Persian authorities therefore forbade the Jews to continue with their work of building. But at the Persian court there was a Jew named Nehemiah, who was 'cup-bearer' to the king—an important and trusted position. He received news that an attack had been made on Jerusalem and the walls had been broken down and the city gates destroyed. He was greatly distressed for, although he had probably never seen Palestine, he thought of Jerusalem as the city of his own people. He put the matter before the king and got permission to visit Jerusalem to put things right. He was given an escort of troops and authority to purchase material for building the city walls. On his arrival he made a personal tour by night around the ruins and next day called on the Jews to set to work.

Opposition soon came from the peoples around. They first laughed at the Jews, declaring that they were trying to build a wall out of a heap of rubbish. They said that if even a fox came up to the wall it would fall down. When this did not deter the builders, their enemies planned an attack, so Nehemiah arranged for guards to be placed while the people were at work, to ward off any assaults. The walls were eventually completed in fifty-two days (October 444 B.C.).

Nehemiah, who had been appointed governor of Jerusalem by the Persians, then set about helping the social and economic life of the Jewish community, to make Judah into a worthy state. He got the wealthy landowners to release the poor people who owed them money, for in some cases these had been made into slaves. He enforced the keeping of the Sabbath, forbidding the Jews to work or trade on that day, and made them promise to give tithes to the priests and pay a tax towards the upkeep of the temple. He found that many Jews had taken foreign wives; even the grandson of the high priest had married the daughter of a man who had opposed Nehemiah's building of the walls. He punished these Jews and forbade the practice of marrying Gentile women.

Nehemiah was governor for about twelve years and his work was later extended by Ezra, who was both a pries and a scribe. He arrived from Persia about 400 B.C., to set the affairs of the Jew in order, for there were reports of disorder and strife. He found that Nehemiah's reforms had not been fully carried out and he made the Jews who had married foreign women divorce their wives. He then ordered the people to assemble in order to hear a reading of the Law—probably the regulations of the book

99

of Deuteronomy—which had been neglected. Finally there was a solemn assembly in which the people bound themselves to the covenant between the nation and God.

Nehemiah and Ezra were largely responsible for making the Jews regard themselves as a distinctive community, separate from and superior to all other nations and races. Their religion tended to be a matter of the observance of legal regulations rather than spiritual fellowship with God. The ideal held out by Deutero-Isaiah, that the Jews might be a missionary people to the world, bringing others to a knowledge of God, was largely forgotten. They came to regard other nations as the enemies of the people of God, to be shunned as far as possible and even despised. There is evidence, however, that some Jews protested against this narrow outlook. One such protest is contained in the book of Jonah.

This book tells a story about a prophet who was commanded by God to journey to Nineveh, the capital of the Assyrian empire, and preach to the people to repent. Jonah shirked his commission and boarded a ship which was going across the Mediterranean, bound for Spain. A storm arose and the superstitious sailors decided that Jonah was responsible for it, so they threw him overboard. A 'great fish' swallowed him and he stayed inside this for three days. At this point the writer of the book inserted a psalm of thanksgiving. Then Jonah was brought out on dry land again. He was once more told to preach to Nineveh and he obeyed, declaring that the city would be destroyed within forty days. Nineveh surprisingly accepted his message and the people, led by the king, repented. So God decided not to punish the city. But Jonah was not at all pleased and was full of self-pity; he had apparently been looking forward to seeing Nineveh destroyed. So he sat down outside the city and sulked. He was still more upset when a large plant with big leaves which had sheltered him from the sun was shrivelled up. The book ends with Yahweh saying that he was in a similar way distressed about Nineveh, where the people had gone astray, and had pity on them, for they were ignorant and innocent.

This book does not relate history. Nineveh never repented and turned to the Hebrew God. It is a work of fiction, written to teach the Jews a lesson. Jonah here represents Israel, which despised the other nations and thought them only deserving of punishment by God— Jonah's attitude towards Nineveh. Like Jonah, the Jews had shirked their duty to give their knowledge of God to others. The stay in the 'great fish' represents the exile of the Jews in Babylon, for a fish or a monster was a common symbol for an empire. The Jews had returned from Babylon and, like Jonah sulking, wanted to keep to themselves. The book is a protest against their spirit of narrow nationalism and a call to remember the teaching of Deutero-Isaiah about the servant of the Lord.

This attitude did not, however, prevail. The Jews followed rather the line laid down by Nehemiah and Ezra. They continue to keep themselves from contact with other nations. Their religious leaders laid stress on the strict observance of the Law, with its numerous regulations which covered all aspects of life. The chief men in the nation were the high priests, who were sometimes unworthy of their office. In spite of these defects, however, the Jews had a religion which was far superior to that of any other people of that time. They were the only monotheists, holding also that Yahweh was a moral God, who wanted a high standard of conduct from his worshippers. The lessons of the prophets such as Amos and Isaiah had at last gone home. There were no great prophets now, however. Their place was taken by the scribes, who copied out the Law and taught it to the people, and by 'wise men', who composed and collected sayings which represented the proverbial wisdom of the race. One such collection is in our Bible—the book of Proverbs—while others are included among Jewish books not in the Old Testament.

There were many Jews living in foreign lands—probably far more numerous than those in Palestine. Large numbers never went back from Babylonia or Persia. There were also Jewish communities in the towns of Asia and in Egypt. These Jews preferred to live in these countries, carrying on trade and other activities. They tended to be more liberal in their outlook than the Palestinian Jews and took a more sympathetic view of Gentile culture. The centre of their religious life was the synagogue, where they could meet and take part in a simple form of worship. But for all the Jews the temple at Jerusalem was their central shrine and those who lived abroad tried to visit it for the great annual festivals.

The historical narratives in the Old Testament finish at this point, about 400 B.C., with Judah a small province of the great Persian empire. For the story of the Jews from that time until the opening of the Christian era we have to turn to other Jewish books and the records of Greek and other historians.

PASSAGES REFERRED TO IN THIS CHAPTER:

Haggai exhorts the Jews to rebuild the temple: *Haggai* 1.1 to 1.7 and 2.1 to 2.5.
The Samaritans offer to help: *Ezra* 4.1 to 4.5.
The Samaritans stop the building of the city walls: *Ezra* 4.7 to 4.23.
Nehemiah receives permission to help Jerusalem: *Nehemiah* 2.1 to 2.18.
The Samaritans oppose his work: *Nehemiah* 4.1 to 4.6 and 4.15 to 4.23.
Ezra reads the Law to the people: *Nehemiah* 8.1 to 8.8.
The story of Jonah: *Jonah* 1 and 3.

10

After the Old Testament

Under the rule of the Persians the Jews had a fairly secure existence. They were allowed religious freedom and were left to develop their national life as long as they paid their taxes and obeyed the commands of their conquerors. Once, about 345 B.C., they joined in a rebellion started by the Phoenicians but the Persians invaded Palestine, put down the revolt and took a large number of the inhabitants of Jerusalem as exiles to Babylon and Persia. However, the Persian empire itself was not to last much longer, for a new power had arisen, this time from Europe, which threatened all the Middle East.

In 336 B.C. a young man named Alexander succeeded to the throne of Greece. His father Philip had been king of Macedonia, a small province in the north, and had established his rule over the whole of Greece. His son was only twenty years old when he inherited this kingdom on his father's death. Revolts broke out in various places in Greece but he soon put these down and then turned his attention eastwards. With his army he crossed over to Asia Minor (Turkey), which was part of the Persian empire, captured a number of towns and defeated the Persian army, led by the emperor Darius himself, at the battle of Issus in 333 B.C. Then he turned south-east,

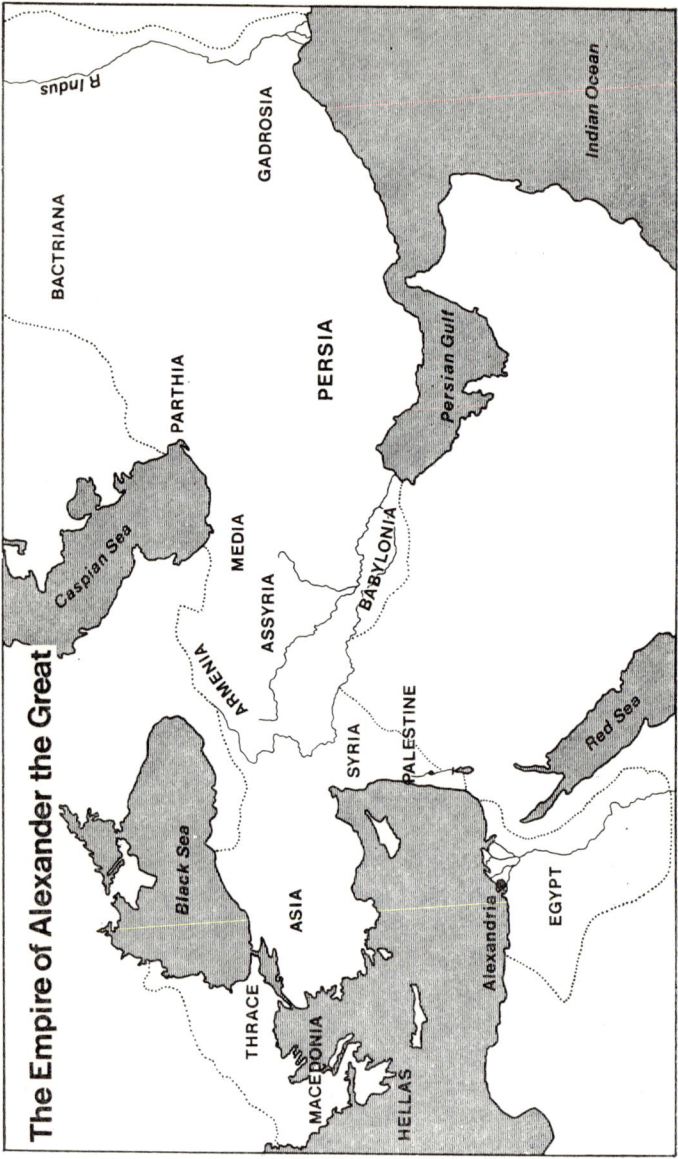

The Empire of Alexander the Great

R Indus

GADROSIA

Indian Ocean

BACTRIANA

PARTHIA

PERSIA

Persian Gulf

MEDIA

ASSYRIA

Caspian Sea

BABYLONIA

ARMENIA

SYRIA

PALESTINE

Red Sea

Black Sea

ASIA

THRACE

MACEDONIA

Alexandria

HELLAS

EGYPT

occupied Syria and Phoenicia and advanced into Palestine. The Samaritans, in the centre of the country, offered him help and in return he gave them permission to build a temple on Mount Gerizim. This increased the bitterness between the Samaritans and the Jews, who held that the only place for sacrifices was at their temple at Jerusalem.

Alexander then moved south to Jerusalem. The city surrendered to him and he continued his triumphant progress to Egypt and subdued that country. He founded the city of Alexandria, named after himself, on the Mediterranean coast and allowed Jews to settle there. Leaving one of his generals in charge, he then turned east once more and led his troops through Palestine towards Mesopotamia. He occupied the territories of the former empires of Assyria and Babylon and marched through Persia to the river Indus on the north-west frontier of India. He returned to Babylon to plan further campaigns but, after a banquet to celebrate his triumphs, caught a chill and died at the age of thirty-two. In a dozen years he had conquered a greater extent of land than any man before him, and his empire stretched for nearly three thousand miles, from west to east. (See map, p. 104.)

When Alexander died in 323 B.C. his empire split up. He had not had time to consolidate his rule but had left the generals of his army in command in different areas. These now set themselves up as rulers and as his successors. Egypt came under a commander named Ptolemy, who after a few years invaded and annexed Palestine. For over a century after this the Jews were ruled from Egypt. The Egyptian monarchs were Greeks, from the line of Ptolemy. During this time the Jews were much influenced by Gentile ideas and customs, which were being spread all over the Middle East as a result of the conquests of Alexander and the Greek colonies he had founded. Greek cities were established even in Palestine. The colony of Jews in Alexandria increased until they eventually numbered about a million. Many of the Jews who lived outside Palestine were unfamiliar with the Hebrew language in which the Old Testament was written. So about 250 B.C. a group of Jewish scribes in Alexandria began to translate their scriptures from Hebrew into Greek. This version of their Bible became known as the Septuagint (abbreviated as LXX), from a tradition that seventy scholars were engaged on it. Actually, different books were translated at various times and the whole work was not completed until many years had passed.

There were also other books, most of them written in Greek, which were produced by Jews living outside Palestine. They are called the Apocrypha (a Greek word meaning hidden, or put aside) for they were not accepted by the Jews of Palestine, who kept only to the books written in Hebrew. Some of the Apocryphal books contain some very fine passages and they are often included (as in the *New English Bible*) between the Old Testament and the New Testament.

In 198 B.C. Palestine came under other kings—the successors of Alexander who ruled at Antioch in Syria. The troops of the Ptolemies were driven out and Jerusalem surrendered to the Syrian armies. The Greek-Syrian king, Antiochus III, treated the Jews well and allowed them religious freedom. The Jews were divided in the attitude they adopted towards the Gentiles under whom they lived and two rival parties arose at Jerusalem. Some Jews, led by a high priest, wished to promote Greek customs and culture. A sports stadium, where athletic contests were held, was built at Jerusalem and Jewish youths took part in the games. Opposing this tendency were Jews who kept to their own religious customs and resisted Greek ways. The great test came when Antiochus IV came to the Syrian throne. He had the title of Epiphanes, which meant that he was a god in human form, and he was determined to make all his empire a united people in culture and religion. He issued a decree that Greek customs and religion were to be observed everywhere.

The Jews were probably the only people in his realm who protested. Antiochus sent an army to attack Jerusalem, which fell easily. The king then forbade all Jewish practices such as the keeping of the Sabbath and the observance of their food laws. All copies of their sacred books that could be found by his officers were burnt. The sacrifices in the temple were stopped. The climax of these measures came in December 168 B.C., when an altar was erected in the temple court to the Greek god Zeus and sacrifice was made on it.

Some of the Jews deserted their principles and tried to keep on the right side of the rulers by adopting Greek ways, but others resisted and refused to take part in the pagan festivals and sacrifices. Men, women and children alike were seized; some were tortured and many were put to death. It looked as if their nation and religion were going to be completely wiped out.

During this time of persecution, the Old Testament book called Daniel was written. The first part contains stories about some Jews who had lived in Babylon during the exile there. On three occasions Daniel and his friends refused to obey the commands of the Babylonian king— that they should eat the food of the royal court instead of their own more simple Jewish diet, that they should worship an image of the Babylonian god and that they should not pray to anybody but the king himself. These stories may have been based on real events in the exile, but the writer told them in order to encourage his fellow Jews in their resistance to the demands of Antiochus Epiphanes. The second part of the book consists of a number of visions which Daniel is said to have had. In these he sees the rise and fall of the empires which in turn had ruled the Jews—the Assyrian, the Babylonian and the Greek, under Alexander, followed by the Syrians under Antiochus. He pictures the downfall of this last oppressor, when God would give authority and power to the Jews who had remained faithful to him. The writer did not refer directly to these empires and rulers, for that would be dangerous if his book should fall into the bands of the Syrian officials, but portrayed them as wild animals such as a lion, leopard or bear. His Jewish readers would recognise these and see what he meant. The book is an example of a type of literature known as 'revelation' (or 'apocalypse', a Greek word meaning 'unveiling'). The writers of such books sought to encourage people who were suffering persecution by unveiling or revealing the future, when their cause would triumph. They put this message forth in a series of visions ascribed to great figures of the past, just as the writer pictured Daniel as foreseeing the plight of the Jews. In this and other ways loyal Jews tried to help those who refused to obey the commands of Antiochus.

The king sent officers through the land to enforce his orders. At the village of Modin, about twenty miles north-west of Jerusalem, the officer set up an altar to the Greek god and called upon an old man named Mattathias to set an example by sacrificing first of all. Mattathias refused and killed the Greek and also a Jew who came forward to sacrifice. This was the signal for a general revolt, which was led by Mattathias' son Judas. He and his brothers trained an army which for three years fought the Syrians. Judas was given the nickname Maccabaeus, which means the Hammerer. Eventually he captured Jerusalem and in December 165 B.C. reconsecrated the temple and restored the Jewish sacrifices. The war against the Syrians continued for some years but eventually the Jews prevailed and the Syrians withdrew.

For about a hundred years the Jews were then independent of foreign control—the first time this had happened since the days of Solomon. They had their own line of kings, from the family of the Maccabees. One of the most outstanding, Simon, brought peace to the land and encouraged the strict observance of their religion. Many of the later kings and priests were unworthy and there was frequent strife between rival parties of Jews, often accompanied by treachery and bloodshed. One of the kings in 110 B.C. destroyed the temple which the Samaritans had set up on Mount Gerizim.

But a new power was advancing from the west, the Romans. During the second and first centuries B.C. these masters of Italy established their rule over almost all the lands bordering on the Mediterranean Sea. In 63 B.C. the Roman general Pompey, a friend at that time of Julius Caesar who set foot on Britain eight years later, had been on a campaign against a king in Asia Minor who had defied the Romans. Then he turned south into Palestine. He advanced to Jerusalem, which surrendered without a fight, but had to besiege the mount on which the temple stood before it could be captured. The Romans generally respected the religion of people whom they conquered and made no attempt to interfere with it. Pompey, however, wanted to see what the God of the Jews was like. In every temple that he knew there were statues of the gods, so he entered the Holy of Holies to satisfy his curiosity. This was of course empty and he came out wondering at this strange people that worshipped an invisible God. He placed the Jews under the rule of the Roman governor of Syria and their period of independence was at an end.

The Romans did not permit the Jews to have a king but they allowed much power to a governor named Antipater, who came from Edom. When he was murdered there was chaos in the country for a few years but his son Herod captured Jerusalem and was installed in 37 B.C. as king of Judea by Mark Antony and Octavian (who later became the first Roman emperor, with the title of

Augustus). Herod was an able monarch and eventually became master of nearly the whole of Palestine. He made Jerusalem a fine city, with a royal palace, and started the building of a new temple, which gradually replaced the one built after the exile. It was begun in 20 B.C. but was not complete until about A.D. 64, long after Herod's death. Despite this the Jews hated him, for he had little real concern for their religious principles and traditions. He favoured Greek ways and had Greek cities built in Palestine. He was a cruel man, responsible for the murder of two high priests, two of his wives (he had ten in all) and three of his sons. It was during his reign that Jesus was born at Bethlehem. The year of his death was what we now call 4 B.C., so our reckoning of the years A.D., supposed to be counted from the birth of Jesus, are some years out—possibly six or eight.

On the death of Herod the Great, as he is generally called, his kingdom was split up among three of his sons. One of them, Archelaus, was given Judea, but was deposed by the Romans after nine years when his subjects complained of the harshness of his rule (A.D. 6). The Romans decided to take over the rule of this part of Palestine themselves and a governor or procurator was appointed over Judea and Samaria. To ensure correct returns for taxation, the Romans held a census. This was resisted by the more strict Jews, to have their numbers counted by a foreign people, and a man named Judas raised a revolt in Galilee. This was crushed mercilessly by the Romans but the followers of Judas continued to plot against the ruling power. They became known as the Zealots. Some of them were called *sicarii*—'dagger men' —for they always held a knife in readiness for an opportunity to use it against the Romans. The Zealots were fanatics from both a political and a religious point of view. Their slogan was: 'No rule but the Law, no king but God'. They held that it was shameful that their nation should be governed by a foreign pagan power and considered that it was the will of God that the conquerors should be resisted and driven out.

There were other Jews who also disliked Roman rule but took no active steps to overthrow it. They showed their loyalty to God not by political action but by religious devotion. They observed the laws and regulations in the Old Testament strictly, as well as additions which had been made by scribes. They considered that when God was satisfied that the nation was keeping the Law he would himself see to the overthrow of their conquerors. Many of these strict Jews belonged to the party of the Pharisees. This name means 'separate' and was used to emphasise that the Jewish nation should be distinct from the Gentiles. The party arose probably in Maccabean times, as a protest against the policy of the priests and leaders of the nation who compromised with Greek ways. The Pharisees had some beliefs which had developed in more recent years and are not mentioned, or are not prominent, in the Old Testament. They looked for a future resurrection of dead people and a day of judgment, when God would deal with men according to their deserts. They also believed that God would send a deliverer, who would be 'anointed' as the kings of the past had been. The Hebrew word for 'anointed' is Messiah, the Greek for which is Christos. This expectation of a Messiah or Christ became general among the Jews and helped to sustain them when they were oppressed. They sometimes referred to the Messiah as 'son of David', as they thought he would be a king like that hero of old.

Another party, which originated about the same time, was that of the Sadducees. Many of these were priests or members of Jewish noble families. They were therefore the ruling party and controlled the Sanhedrin—a court of justice which had the right to try offences against the Jewish religious or national laws. The Romans often allowed nations under their rule to keep their own form of government, provided they did not oppose the Roman governor or stir up trouble. The Sadducees accepted only the books of the Law in the Old Testament and rejected the teaching of the prophets and later ideas such as a resurrection of the dead. They had no interest in the expectation of a Messiah. As they controlled the temple— the high priest was a Sadducee—and held the chief offices in the nation, they felt bound to keep on the right side of the Romans, so they generally worked along with them. They regarded with distaste or horror the agitations of the Zealots.

The common people of Palestine belonged to none of these parties. They hated the Romans but realised that they had to put up with their rule. They tried to observe their religious duties and to worship God faithfully in the synagogues. These buildings were now to be found all over Palestine and in many places in the Roman empire, wherever there were at least a dozen Jews. The synagogue was their place of worship on the Sabbath and a school for the Jewish boys was held there during the week. No sacrifices were performed in the synagogue and priests had no official position there. Elders or rulers of the synagogue, who were men of importance and influence in the local community, were in charge and the synagogue became the centre of the religious and social life of the Jews.

The temple at Jerusalem was quite different. Herod's temple was a magnificent affair. It was built of white stone and the roof was plated with gold. The temple building itself was a comparatively small structure, into which only priests went. The innermost shrine, the Holy of Holies, was entered only by the high priest on one day in the year—the Day of Atonement, in the early autumn, when he went inside to make confession of the sins of the people. Outside the building there was a Court of the

Priests, where sacrifices were made on the altars and, further to the east, two open courtyards where only Jews were allowed. Surrounding the whole area was a very large Court of the Gentiles, into which anybody of any race could go. There were sacrifices of animals in the Priests' Court every day, at morning and late afternoon, and pilgrims from all over the Roman world used to visit the temple for the great festivals of the Jewish year.

It was in this situation that Jesus of Nazareth lived and taught—in a country where there was bitter political and religious argument between rival parties, where the people either suffered in silence, depressed and confused, or broke out into violent revolt against an oppressive foreign power. This explains why he was put to death by the Romans. The Jewish priests were against him because they thought he was attacking their privileged position and wanted to be the Messiah, and they brought him before the Roman procurator, Pontius Pilate, accusing him of stirring up the people and claiming to be a king. The Romans would not allow anybody to be a king without their consent, so Pilate had him executed by the Roman method of crucifixion.

After the death of Jesus (about A.D. 30) the country became more and more disturbed. Any signs of revolt were crushed mercilessly by the Roman governors. The procurator Gessius Florus, who was appointed in A.D. 64, was a cruel man, who encouraged the murder of his opponents, robbed the Jews and plundered their cities. Eventually the Jews could stand it no longer. A riot broke out in Jerusalem and the Roman garrison was attacked. The Pharisees and the priests joined in trying to persuade the people against the foolishness of resistance, but the Zealots had their way. They stirred up the people throughout the country against the Romans. The Roman emperor sent the general, Vespasian, to Palestine and he put down revolts which had broken out in Galilee. Then he set out to besiege Jerusalem. The Jews defending the city were in a terrible plight; the inhabitants not only suffered from famine as a result of the siege but there were quarrels between different parties of Zealots, who fought one another as fiercely as they tried to repel the Romans. The city finally fell to Titus, the son of Vespasian, in August, A.D. 70. The Romans wiped out the remaining defenders and burnt the temple of Herod. Resistance continued for another three years, from a band of Zealots who had seized the fortress of Masada, overlooking the Dead Sea. When the Romans stormed it in A.D. 73 they found all the garrison of over 900 men dead.

In A.D. 70 the Jewish nation, therefore, ceased to exist. The Romans incorporated Judea into the province of Syria. There was one more attempt by the Jews to regain their independence. In the years 132–135 there was another revolt in Palestine, led by a man who claimed to be the Messiah, Bar-Cochba. The Romans crushed this last outburst of Zealot fury. Cities and villages were destroyed and thousands of rebels were slaughtered in battle. The countryside was devastated and nothing was left of the old city of Jerusalem. The emperor Hadrian gave orders for a Roman city to be built on the site.

But Judaism, the religion and way of life of the Jews, did not die. This was because Jews were now to be found in almost every part of the Roman world. They kept true to their religion and after the temple had been wiped out they turned with greater devotion to the worship and instruction in the synagogues and the observance of the Law in their private lives. They continued to be a people with a distinctive message for the world, although they were no longer a nation. The race had travelled a long way since Abraham, whom they hailed as their father, had set out as a nomad to wander to Canaan. But they still held fast to the covenant which had been made by their lawgiver Moses and the teaching of the prophets.

The Lord was their God and they were his people. They were the only people in the Roman world who believed in ethical monotheism—that there was only one God and that he wanted from his worshippers an upright life, high moral standards and a regard for other people. The heart of Judaism is well summed up in two commandments in the Old Testament, which Jesus quoted: 'You must love God with all your heart and soul and mind and strength' and 'You must love your neighbour as yourself'.

PASSAGES REFERRED TO IN THIS CHAPTER:

Stories told to encourage the Jews under persecution:

Daniel and his friends defy the Babylonian king: *Daniel* 1.

Three Jews refuse to worship the king's image: *Daniel* 3.

Daniel refuses to give up his prayers: *Daniel* 6.

The fight of the Maccabees:

The decree of Antiochus: 1 *Maccabees* 1.41 to 1.64.

The defiance of Mattathias: 1 *Maccabees* 2.15 to 2.28.

The rededication of the temple: 1 *Maccabees* 4.36 to 4.61.

Other passages from the Apocrypha:

The future of the righteous: *Wisdom of Solomon*: 3.1 to 3.9.

The praise of wisdom: *Wisdom of Solomon* 6.12 to 6.25.

The origin of true wisdom: *Ecclesiasticus* (the wisdom of Jesus, son of Sirach) 1.1 to 1.10.

The praise of famous men: *Ecclesiasticus* 44.

Important Dates

B.C.

About 1700	Abraham in Canaan.
About 1250	The Exodus from Egypt. Moses.
About 1030	Saul, the first Hebrew king.
About 1010	David king of Israel.
About 970	Death of Solomon. Division of the kingdom.
About 850	Ahab king of Israel. Elijah.
About 750	Amos and Hosea in Israel.
740–701	Isaiah in Jerusalem.
722	The fall of Samaria to the Assyrians. End of the northern kingdom.
627–586	Jeremiah in Jerusalem.
586	Capture of Jerusalem by Nebuchadrezzar. Beginning of the exile.
	Ezekiel and Deutero-Isaiah in Babylon.
538	Return of Jews from exile.
444–400	Nehemiah and Ezra in Jerusalem.
323	Capture of Jerusalem by Alexander the Great.
168–165	Campaign of the Maccabees.
63	Capture of Jerusalem by Pompey.
37	Herod king of the Jews.

A.D.

About 30	The crucifixion of Jesus of Nazareth.
70	Capture of Jerusalem by Titus. Destruction of the temple.
132–135	Revolt of Bar-Cochba. Final destruction of Jerusalem.

Index

13